LANGUAGE AND LITERACY SERIES

Dorothy S. Strickland, FOUNDING
Celia Genishi and Donna E. Alverman

D0497427

(continued)

Learning from Culturally and Linguistically Diverse Classrooms

Using Inquiry to Inform Practice

EDITED BY

Joan C. Fingon
Sharon H. Ulanoff

Foreword by Douglas Fisher

Teachers College, Columbia University
New York and London

Published by Teachers College Press, 1234 Amsterdam Avenue, New York, NY
10027

Library of Congress Cataloging-in-Publication Data

Learning from culturally and linguistically diverse classrooms : using inquiry to
  inform practice / edited by Joan C. Fingon, Sharon H. Ulanoff ; foreword by
  Douglas Fisher.
    p. cm.
  ISBN 978-0-8077-5344-6 (pbk. : alk. paper)—ISBN 978-0-8077-5345-3
  (hardcover : alk. paper)
  1. English language—Study and teaching (Elementary)—Foreign speakers.
  2. English language—Study and teaching (Elementary)—United States.
  3. Language arts (Elementary)—Social aspects. 4. Literacy—Social aspects.
  I. Fingon, Joan C. II. Ulanoff, Sharon H.
  PE1128.A2L368 2012
  372.65′0440973—dc23   2012014362

ISBN 978-0-8077-5344-6 (paperback)
ISBN 978-0-8077-5345-3 (hardcover)

Printed on acid-free paper
Manufactured in the United States of America

19   18   17   16   15   14   13   12   8   7   6   5   4   3   2   1

To my mother Claire and my children, Shallon and Collin, who have been my motivation and inspiration along the way, and to Michael for his endearing patience and support.

—Joan C. Fingon

In memory of my parents, Fannie and Harry, I miss you more than you know; and to my students, who continue to inspire and teach me everyday. Thanks again to Mary Lou for still bringing chocolate.

—Sharon H. Ulanoff

Contents

Foreword

What might we see if we entered a classroom? Would we see what we expected to see or would we see something else? How are our expectations for quality instruction formed? In other words, is what we expect to see when we enter a classroom reasonable and based on the best evidence for effectiveness? Further, how might we research what we see in a classroom and even change the practices of teachers through our research? These are the questions that are answered in this book. The authors and editors of *Learning from Culturally and Linguistically Diverse Classrooms: Using Inquiry to Improve Practice* take us inside classrooms and help us identify what quality instruction for diverse learners should look like. To my thinking, there are three unique contributions this book makes.

First, it is clear that interactions matter. Diverse learners simply must interact with one another and the content if they are to be successful in school and beyond. It seems to me that there are too many classrooms in which students are expected to listen for long periods of time. In those classrooms, students develop their listening skills, but teachers and administrators are amazed that they don't develop their reading, writing, and speaking skills. It's pretty simple—you don't get good at something you don't do. As highlighted several times in this book, students need opportunities to interact, using academic language and the language of instruction. These interactions provide students with language practice. What's even more important is talking and thinking with other people to develop their understanding of the world. For example, I have personally never seen the great pyramids of Egypt, even though I would love to. I have had opportunities to read about them and thus have a passing knowledge of their magnificence. But sitting next to a person on a plane who talked with me about his experience and showed me pictures on his iPhone expanded my understanding of this world wonder. I have more background knowledge as a result of that interaction and can use that knowledge in my future reading, writing, and speaking tasks. This interaction also motivated me to learn more, so I downloaded a few books on my iPad to do just that. My experience is not unique. Interactions change us all. As the chapters in this book suggest, we can provide multiple and varied opportunities for students to interact. When students have the opportunity to interact, they learn more. They are also motivated to keep learning.

Second, I was struck by the focus in this book on classroom structures. There are structures that work, and there are those that do not work. Researchers and teachers have uncovered a number of structures that positively impact student learning and they are profiled in this book. I appreciate the focus on effective structures and the clear implications for teaching and researching classrooms of the future. It's not scripted lessons in which teachers read from published curriculum but rather thoughtful and planned instruction and intervention that results in the learning profiled in this book. I noted that, in addition to student interaction, there is evidence for teacher modeling and scaffolding, guided learning, and independent work. In essence, the teachers profiled in this book have identified ways to facilitate student learning without teaching to the middle and leaving some students behind. They are lead learners themselves and meet students where they are while simultaneously holding high expectations for achievement. This balancing act, evident and exemplified in each chapter, requires extensive teacher knowledge and expertise and brings joy to teaching.

Further, and perhaps why this book makes a unique contribution, there are a number of research tools embedded in each chapter of this book. As teachers, we can use these tools to investigate our own classrooms. The teacher as researcher is an appropriate metaphor. As teachers, we should continually investigate our classrooms and our practices. We have to study every aspect of what we do, reflect on that data, and make changes accordingly. We are never finished, because there are always new students with unique backgrounds who want to learn with us. Adopting the stance portrayed in this book—that research informs us at every level—is critical if teachers and schools are to move beyond the "assign-define-test" curriculum that has become prevalent under the "raise test scores" movement. Yes, we can improve student learning, motivation, engagement, and passion, but to do so requires that we learn to examine our practices and make changes accordingly. The teachers profiled in this book know that. They are clearly very good at what they do, *and* they know that they must change to address the diverse needs of their learners. Enjoy this book as much as I did.

—*Douglas Fisher, San Diego State University*

Making Meaning of Classroom Research

Joan C. Fingon
Sharon H. Ulanoff

As public schools in the United States become increasingly diverse, classroom teachers are presented with many challenges. Largely due to state and federal mandates, teachers are being held accountable for increasing reading achievement for all children, including students with diverse needs. While progress and trends have been disputed, certain subgroups lag behind, which has been a preoccupation of educators and politicians alike (Allington, 2012; Santamaría, 2009). According to the 2009 National Assessment of Educational Progress (NAEP) results (NCES, 2009; Vanneman, Baldwin Anderson, & Rahman, 2009) there is a 25-point gap between Black and White fourth-grade reading scores and a 26-point gap at eighth grade. Similarly, some states including California had larger achievement gaps in 2009 between Latino and White students in fourth-grade reading (Vanneman, Baldwin Anderson, & Rahman, 2009). More important, over time the overall gain in the NAEP fourth-grade trend data shows an average reading improvement of only 12 points between 1979 and 2009 and a meager gain of 5 points since 1980 (Allington, 2012). Clearly, as classroom demographics shift, decreasing the achievement gap between groups continues to be a priority.

Continually thinking about how to help our graduate students in teacher education better meet the needs of their students, we got the idea for this book when we were trying to find a new text for a course in literacy research that we teach. The course is part of a Masters in Education program, with an option in Reading, in the large urban university where we teach. In particular, we wanted a text that not only *showed* our students what reading research looked like, but that also could serve as a guide to help our students *conduct* reading research in their own classrooms. Because much of what we believe in and practice ourselves compels us to instill in our students the value and ideals of learning, doing, and teaching in the context of classroom research, we engaged in an ongoing search for readings that would model our beliefs. Because most of our graduate students work in urban public schools teaching predominantly culturally and linguistically diverse learners, we were also looking for a text that featured research in classrooms with learners similar to the ones they teach.

As volume editors and chapter authors, we bring more than three decades of work in K–12 and university classrooms to our roles as teacher educators. We also share a passion about teaching and doing classroom research and about how the two are inextricably linked (Ulanoff, Vega-Castaneda, & Quiocho, 2003). Besides our joint and individual research projects, we share a vision to teach, inspire, and motivate students in the aforementioned core reading research course that we both teach. Over the years, we have used a number of good texts for the course but have always struggled to find a book that focused on new classroom research based on the contexts of the schools and students in which our graduate students teach. We were also interested in knowing what some of our colleagues in California and other parts of the country were learning about K–12 students' literacy development in diverse and changing contexts as they engaged in their own inquiries about literacy practices. Throughout this process, we kept returning to a discussion surrounding an appropriate text for our course, trying out a variety of different ones but always supplementing those works to focus attention on culturally and linguistically diverse learners.

As often happens during such discussions, we considered putting together our own text that not only would address the kinds of classroom research in reading we wanted for our graduate students, but would also highlight new classroom-based reading research in diverse classrooms. Along with our own work, we invited several colleagues to contribute chapters describing their own research in K–12 classrooms.

Rather than look at "one-size-fits-all" types of quick fixes to raise achievement scores (Allington & Cunningham, 2002), we set out to include a more descriptive look at what is going on in classrooms to serve as a resource for classroom teachers, reading specialists, literacy coaches, reading curriculum coordinators, and other educators. Our hope is that by looking within classrooms we can promote professional conversations to initiate change in instructional literacy practices and educational outcomes for all children. The chapters presented in this text span age groups and grade levels from preschool through high school, focusing on instructional practices that support students in predominantly culturally and linguistically diverse classrooms. Thus the book's goals are two-fold:

- To explore classrooms where teachers provide effective instruction for diverse learners
- To demonstrate how teachers and researchers go about conducting inquiries to "capture instructional practices"

More important, this book highlights research that shows how instruction can build on English language learners' (ELLs) English language development (ELD) while respecting and expressing students' linguistic and cultural differences in learning English. The book also aims to underscore the critical roles that literacy and language development play within the context of culturally and linguistically diverse learning related to the intersection of literacy research that is situated in the multiple language and literacy contexts that are experienced by ELLs and the broader context of diverse groups of students.

While much information regarding the best ways to teach all students can be gleaned from federally funded longitudinal or cross-sectional studies of classroom practices and student outcomes, researchers who go into individual classrooms to conduct in-depth studies of instructional practice can serve to clarify, augment, and pose questions about findings of large-scale studies. Many researchers (Cochran-Smith, 1995; Cochran-Smith & Lytle, 1999; Fecho, 2003) have described the need for "practitioner research" that helps teachers better understand, not only the students they teach and their roles as teachers, but also the connections between theory and practice. Therefore, our aim is to describe what classroom research looks like steeped in the same underlying theoretical framework based on best practices for diverse learners. Thus we present inquiries situated within everyday classroom settings that highlight practices similar to those our graduate students see within the contexts of their own classrooms or schools. While we agree that there is no singular or perfect way to help those who teach culturally and linguistically diverse students, the chapters in this book emphasize practical research implications and meaningful lessons learned from working in classrooms.

We want the book to serve as a springboard for ongoing dialogue both about the findings and implications of the studies and about the processes involved in conducting classroom research in valid and reliable ways. In their book on observational research Waxman, Hilberg, and Tharp (2004) point out several educational purposes for systematic classroom observations, including "describing instructional practices, investigating instructional inequities for different groups of students . . . and improving teachers' classroom instruction based on feedback from individual classroom profiles" (pp. 273–274). We argue that those educational purposes can be well served by examining classroom research that explores the ways in which instructional contexts support learning for all students and suggest that the studies in this book will assist educators in understanding the importance of effective work in schools.

HOW WE TEACH ABOUT INQUIRY

Before writing this introduction we spent some time reflecting on how we first began teaching our reading research classes, selecting our readings, and developing assignments in ways that would benefit our students. Personally and professionally, we both believe that students profit most from not only understanding research results by reflecting and thinking critically, but also from understanding the process of how classroom research works. In addition, we believe students need opportunities to ask questions and make connections between what they know and what they are learning in order to enhance their overall understanding of research practices. As William Butler Yeats once said, "Education is not the filling of a pail but the lighting of a fire." Thus our aim is to instill in others curiosity or "the lighting of the fire" to explore and engage in classroom literacy research.

In our classes we emphasize the notion of inquiry-based instruction (Harste, 1993, 2001) as both a means of moving our students—all of them teachers—toward developing an *inquiry ethic* and also as one way to model such instruction as a means of promoting its usage in their own practice. We ask our students to pose their own questions in order that they may plan and implement research to examine answers to those questions (Rosebery, Warren, & Conant, 1992). We want our students to be reflective practitioners (Schön, 1983; Zeichner & Liston, 1996) and engage in *inquiry as stance* (Cochran-Smith & Lytle, 1999, 2009; Ulanoff et al., 2003), asking questions about their own teaching practices in order to promote change.

At the beginning of the course we activate or trigger students' schema and background knowledge by providing a series of questions for them to discuss in small groups about their knowledge, skills, and ability related to classroom research and inquiry-based instruction.

FIGURE I.1. Questions for Discussion
_____

Student Values and Beliefs About Classroom Research

1. What is your current understanding of classroom research? Do
    you know anyone who has conducted research or have you ever
    participated in a research project?
2. How confident are you in your knowledge, skills, and ability to conduct
    classroom research of your own at this time?
3. What benefits or value do you see in becoming involved in classroom
    research?
4. How often do you reflect on your own teaching practices? Describe
    your current approach or the processes that you use and why.
5. What different literacy strategies based on students' diverse cultural
    and linguistic needs have you observed or read about?
6. What are some ways you think you can build on your own
    understanding and develop your own inquiry as stance (as discussed in
    Cochran-Smith & Lytle, 2009)?
_____

After they dialogue in small groups, we share their perceptions and
assumptions about the value and benefits of doing classroom research
in class. Some examples of questions we use to initiate discussion at
the beginning of the course are offered in Figure I.1.

Three Axioms for Classroom Research

In addition to these initial questions, we have coupled other questions that we use while students engage in coursework based on three
truisms, or axioms, that we call "Three Axioms for Classroom Research: Learning by Connecting, Learning by Inquiring and Reflecting, and Learning by Doing Research" (see Figure I.2). All questions
are designed with the purpose of helping students as they begin thinking about and developing the habit of making connections, posing
questions and reflecting on what they know, and linking theory to
practice. However, these questions could also benefit others who already have experience or are interested in knowing more about or
strengthening their understanding of classroom research. While the
questions have been arranged into three sections, they are not meant
to be linear and can be used interchangeably or modified for chapter
readings as necessary

    Axiom One: Learning by Connecting. In the first classroom research
axiom the questions are meant to be a jumping-off point to help stu-

FIGURE I.2. Three Axioms for Classroom Research

Axiom One: Learning by Connecting

1. In your own words, describe your understanding of the relevance and importance of the topic and major concepts presented in this chapter.
2. What underlying assumptions, perceptions, and beliefs did you have about classroom research and diverse learners prior to reading this chapter? Did your ideas change? Why or why not?
3. How would you describe the spectrum of learners in this chapter? How does the context of the study compare or contrast to your students and your school environment?
4. How does the classroom research presented in this chapter help clarify, augment, or raise questions about findings of large-scale studies? Explain your point of view.
5. Describe how the authors or researchers went about conducting inquiries to capture instructional practices in this chapter.
6. How realistic or practical are the findings or implications? Explain your reasons.

Axiom Two: Learning by Inquiring and Reflecting

1. What critical, burning, or essential questions or ideas surfaced for you after reading the chapter?
2. How did this chapter enhance your understanding or level of awareness of students you teach and of your role as a teacher?
3. What political, cultural, social, and economical factors do you think also contribute to or influence the research and ideas presented in this chapter?
4. What discoveries or connections have you made between theory and practice?
5. What questions do you have for the authors or researchers about their findings and research implications?
6. Has your thinking related to the ideas or research presented changed after reading this chapter? Why or why not?
7. Briefly describe your current understanding of inquiry as stance. What ideas emerged for you in the chapter to help you become a more reflective practitioner?

Axiom Three: Learning by Doing Research

1. What ideas have you identified about conducting research of your own related to the concepts presented in this chapter?
2. How might you apply what you have read to benefit your own research and students in your teaching situation?
3. What questions might you pose about initiating your own classroom research?
4. How would you go about designing your own research and what would it look like?

dents understand, clarify, and make personal connections to the content in the course readings. These questions can be used as a guide to initiate dialogue in small groups or in whole-class discussion. They can also help enhance students' level of awareness and understanding of the contexts of their own teaching and learning experiences.

Axiom Two: Learning by Inquiring and Reflecting. This axiom includes questions to facilitate discussion and help students share their own ideas and inquiry beyond the content of the specific reading as they begin to relate to further implications for the field. These questions also build upon questions provided in the first axiom in helping students formulate their own inquiry and research related to their own teaching practices.

Axiom Three: Learning by Doing Research. The third axiom asks students to pull together their own ideas and ways they may go about designing their own classroom research related to their students and the role they play in improving students' literacy development. These questions can serve as a framework to help students as they begin investigating their own research questions and research design about what they want to know or what is important to them in their own instructional practices.

Weekly Reflections

Another way we help our students make meaning of classroom research involves writing weekly reflections, understanding that the *art of reflection* is something that must also be taught. Our use of weekly reflections is guided by the research on reflective judgment (King & Kitchener, 1994) and deeply connected to our belief in the linkage between reflection and teacher self-efficacy (Bandura, 1997; Tschannen-Moran & Woolfolk Hoy, 2006). Since we believe that reflection and inquiry are the heart of learning, we use tools such as reader response logs and dialectical journals that have proven to be successful with students. We present students with two different reflection templates (see Figures I.3 and I.4 for examples) and ask them to choose a version to complete after reading a required book chapter as well as other selected research articles assigned on a weekly basis. We also give our students the option of developing their own reflection template.

By assigning purposeful and thought-provoking readings on research, we give students opportunities to think critically and formulate their thoughts by writing down their ideas, posing questions, and

FIGURE I.3. Responding to Readings

Reader Response Log Template

Student name _____**Date** _____

Chapter title/article _____

1. What key concepts, theories, or ideas have you identified from the chapter?
2. List several important or relevant quotations of interest and tell why you selected them (include chapter and page numbers).
3. What are your connections to the readings based on your teaching and overall school experiences?
4. What implications does this chapter offer to help your own students and instructional practices?
5. What questions do you have about the readings for small-group or whole-class discussion?

making connections to their own teaching and learning experiences, as well as by developing their own inquiry ethic (Ulanoff et al., 2003). We believe students need ample opportunities to write, read, reflect, and engage in discussion about classroom research so they can construct research questions about their own teaching. We also model by posing questions related to our own classroom research projects that we are conducting with our students. In addition, as students begin the process of posing and constructing questions about their own teaching practices and classroom research, we provide ongoing feedback to expand and support their ideas.

We have found both the reader response logs and the dialectical journals successful in ways that support teachers' learning and understanding of classroom research and inquiry-based learning. We invite you to try either template or adapt and modify the questions as needed to meet your students' needs.

Expanding Students' Inquiry Learning

Other assignments that help improve students' research knowledge base include having them prepare a review of the literature on a research topic of their choice. The intent of this assignment is to help

FIGURE I.4. Journaling About Research

Dialectical Journal Template

Student name _____

Chapter title/article _____

Criteria	My Ideas from the Readings
Key concepts, theories, or ideas gathered from the chapter.	
My important or relevant quotations of interest and rationale for selecting them (include page #s).	
My connections to the readings based on my teaching and overall background and schooling experiences.	
My understanding and questions of research implications or lessons learned from the chapter.	
My questions for the author(s) or about the research topic.	

students develop a theoretical framework as they prepare their own classroom research proposal to carry out during the term. As a culminating project, we have them conduct a small field-research or inquiry project to answer critical questions about literacy instruction in their own classrooms. We ask students to share their research findings in small groups by preparing oral presentations in class. Throughout the course we also assess students' contributions to thinking in class, interaction with their peers, critical analysis of their own ideas and questions raised of the readings based on responses in their reader response logs or dialectical journals, and their overall contribution to supporting and evaluating others during individual or small-group oral presentations.

ORGANIZATION OF THE BOOK

We carefully selected the authors for this book based on their passion, expertise, and impressive activity in the field of classroom literacy research. We wanted classroom researchers who were able to model as well as articulate and elaborate on their research views related to diverse learners at various grade levels (from preschool through older students) and from around the country. Chapter 1, by Joan C. Fingon, examines the common widespread practice of mandating "core" reading programs in public schools for all students and the urgency to explore and improve those practices. It examines the connections between teachers' beliefs and practices related to an evaluation of a K–12 districtwide reading program and how teachers work within the constraints of implementing a core reading program with limited numbers of English language learners. In Chapter 2 Virginia Gonzalez demonstrates the link between first and second language and literacy development of Hispanic immigrant preschoolers enrolled in a bilingual developmental preschool Head Start program. In Chapter 3 Sharon H. Ulanoff, Ambika G. Raj, Diane Brantley, Susan Courtney, and Richard Rogers take us into a K–2 multiage classroom in central Los Angeles, where two teachers work within the constraints of mandated curriculum, a scripted reading program, and rigid pacing plans to create spaces where second language learners not only learn, they thrive.

In Chapter 4 Jodene Kersten Morrell brings us into a fourth-grade classroom to look at the ways in which her work in an after-school young writers' group positively impacted the Latino students' literacy learning in their classrooms. In Chapter 5 Alice Quiocho and Sharon H. Ulanoff follow with an in-depth look at how a fourth-grade teacher and literacy coach collaborated to develop writing instruction that not only connected to the students' social studies and science content, but also allowed them to take risks with language in ways that enhanced their literacy skills. Next, in Chapter 6, Shira Lubliner and Dana L. Grisham take us into a fifth-grade classroom to demonstrate how the use of cognate strategy instruction with Spanish-speaking English learners impacted their literacy development. Also working with fifth graders, Sandra A. Butvilofsky looks at bilingual students' perceptions of the functions of Spanish and English as they learn to read and write simultaneously in both languages in Chapter 7.

Linking social studies to vocabulary development and reading comprehension in Chapter 8, Josephine Arce and Elizabeth Padilla Detwiler demonstrate how eighth-grade ELLs who engage in content-based discussions can improve both oral language and literacy development. Finally, in Chapter 9, Sandra Liliana Pucci and Gregory J. Cramer describe how one small Midwestern high school, an "instrumentality charter school" that based its instruction on the principles of biliteracy development, worked to support its diverse student body and promote academic success. In the Afterword, Joan C. Fingon and Sharon H. Ulanoff offer suggestions for school change to support and encourage educators in developing their own inquiry skills and research agenda to improve literacy achievement for all students.

PARTING THOUGHTS

The current political and educational climate seems ripe for rich conversations about developing better schools for all students, including diverse learners. Allington and Cunningham (2002) offer these ideas about school reform: "Schools that work for all children are not the product of a state-mandated school improvement plan or the result of a federal program grant or a plan developed and mandated by district office personnel. Schools are changed by the people who work in them" (p. 282). We hope that educators who are interested in developing an inquiry ethic and engaging in literacy research find the research axioms (Learning by Connecting, Learning by Inquiring and Reflecting, and Learning by Doing Research) useful and the reflection tools helpful in guiding student researchers. More important, we hope that the classroom research presented by the authors in this book helps stimulate continuing conversations.

REFERENCES

Allington, R. L. (2012). *What really matters for struggling readers: Designing research-based programs.* Boston, MA: Pearson.

Allington, R. L., & Cunningham, P. M. (2002). *Schools that work: Where all children read and write.* Boston, MA: Allyn & Bacon.

Bandura, A. (1997). *Self-efficacy: The exercise of control.* New York, NY: W. H. Freeman.

Cochran-Smith, M. (1995). Color blindness and basket making are not the answers: Confronting the dilemmas of race, culture, and language diversity in teacher education. *American Educational Research Journal, 32*(3), 493–522.

Cochran-Smith, M., & Lytle, S. L. (1999). The teacher research movement: A decade later. *Educational Researcher, 28*(7), 15–25.

Cochran-Smith, M., & Lytle, S. L. (2009). *Inquiry as stance: Practitioner research in the next generation.* New York, NY: Teachers College Press.

Fecho, B. (2003). Yeki bood/Yeki na bood: Writing and publishing as a teacher researcher. *Research in the Teaching of English, 37*(3), 281–294.

Harste, J. (1993). Inquiry-based instruction. *Primary Voices K–6, 1,* 2–5.

Harste, J. (2001). What education as inquiry is and isn't. In S. Boran & B. Comber (Eds.), *Critiquing whole language and classroom inquiry.* Urbana, IL: National Council of Teachers of English.

King, P. M., & Kitchener, K. S. (1994). Developing reflective judgment: Understanding and promoting intellectual growth and critical thinking in adolescents and adults. San Francisco, CA: Jossey-Bass.

National Center for Education Statistics (NCES). (2009). *NAEP data explorer: National Assessment of Educational Progress 2009 reading assessment.* Retrieved from http://nces.ed.gov/nationsreportcard/NDEHelp/WebHelp/welcome_to_ the_naep_data_explorer.htm

Rosebery, A. S., Warren, B., & Conant, F. R. (1992). *Appropriating scientific discourse: Findings from language minority classrooms.* Santa Cruz, CA: National Center for Research on Cultural Diversity and Second Language Learning.

Schön, D. A. (1983). *The reflective practitioner: How professionals think in action.* New York, NY: Basic Books.

Santamaría, L. J. (2009). Culturally responsive differentiated instruction: Narrowing gaps between best pedagogical practices benefiting all learners, *Teachers College Record, 111,* 214–247.

Tschannen-Moran, M., & Woolfolk Hoy, A. (2006). Teacher efficacy: Capturing an elusive construct. *Teaching and Teacher Education, 17,* 783–805.

Ulanoff, S. H., Vega-Castaneda, L., & Quiocho, A. M. L. (2003). Teachers as researchers: Developing an inquiry ethic. *Teacher Development, 7*(3), 403–436.

Vanneman, A., Baldwin Anderson, J., & Rahman, T .(2009). *Achievement gaps: How Black and White students in public schools perform in mathematics and reading on the NEAP* (NCES 2009-455) Washington, DC: National Center for Education Statistics and Educational Sciences, U.S. Dept. of Education.

Waxman, H. C., Hilberg, R. S., & Tharp, R. G. (2004). Future directions for classroom observational research. In H. C. Waxman, R. G. Tharp, & R. S. Hilberg (Eds.), *Observational research in U.S. classrooms: New approaches for understanding cultural and linguistic diversity* (pp. 266–277). New York, NY: Cambridge University Press.

Zeichner, K. M., & Liston, D. P. (1996). *Reflective teaching: An introduction.* Mahwah, NJ: Lawrence Erlbaum.

CHAPTER 1

Honoring Teacher Voices

Practices and Perceptions of Teachers Using a Core Reading Program to Support School Improvement

Joan C. Fingon

In most public school systems across America core reading programs (CRPs) have become a focal point for reading instruction. One issue encompassing the widespread practice of using CRPs includes the remarkable variance of teachers' beliefs and instructional practices during program implementation. Comments made during a curriculum meeting by two elementary teachers who work in the same school and grade level and use the same program bring this matter to light:

> *Teacher 1:* I like the structure of the program and follow the lesson plans step-by-step. I have more confidence in my teaching because of the design of the program. My students enjoy using the materials.

> *Teacher 2:* The program is too rigid. I've been at this for a long time. It seems that among us we believe the reading program is not for everybody but it's delivered to everyone. This doesn't make sense!

Within the context of today's call for more accountability for teaching children, states, districts, and schools are adopting and/or "mandating" that teachers use CRPs to guide instruction for all. CRPs consist of a systematized set of instructional materials or program that teachers use to teach children to learn to read. CRPs are comprehensive in nature, "providing a structure for organizing time, texts, and teaching strategies" (Dewitz, Leahy, Jones, & Maslin Sullivan, 2010, p. 281). They are generally written, produced, and marketed by program developers and consultants who provide a mixture of resources and materials adopted or mandated by many public schools for reading instruction (Dewitz, Jones, & Leahy, 2009). Serving as the base for reading instruction, the expectation is that teachers implement the program to address the needs of most students in the classroom. However, when schools sanction a method or program to be taught to all students in the same way, teachers may not always agree with nor may all students benefit from that program or model. Moreover, while other materials and resources can be used, most schools tend to rely on one program as their primary source for reading instruction. Although CRPs are not new and their effectiveness has been debated for years, they continue to have much influence and control over reading instruction (Brenner & Hiebert, 2010).

To extend this conversation, one must acknowledge that CRPs are embedded in a multitude of factors including current legislative priorities such as No Child Left Behind (NCLB, 2002), state and district policies, commercial program publishers' influences, and prevailing views of leading experts in the field of reading research. Since CRPs are designed to provide a series of lessons, strategies, and resources, they may not always offer enough support for instruction, particularly for culturally and linguistically diverse or lowest performing students. For example, while students have shown some growth in reading skills as measured by the National Assessment of Educational Progress (NAEP), scores for students from diverse backgrounds and English language learners (ELLs) have shown little improvement since 1991 (NCES, 2011). Furthermore, since 2007 there has been little change in reading score gaps between groups based on race/ethnicity, gender, or school type, with the exception of a slight narrowing between White and Black students in Grade 4 and females and males in Grade 8 (NCES, 2009). Adding the media's focus and the general public's perception that schools are lacking, it is no wonder teachers are feeling caught between deciding if teaching has more to do with complying with mandated curricula than with meeting students' individual needs.

As CRPs continue to be a major focus in reading instruction, we can learn a lot by listening to teachers' views and opinions related to how they employ such program lessons, materials, and strategies to meet student's needs. Moreover, because students do not learn in the same way, teachers do not teach the same way for various reasons (Allington, 2012).

THE ROLE OF CORE READING PROGRAMS IN SCHOOLS

In order to explore the issue of successful reading instruction, I conducted an evaluation of a CRP in a centralized urban public school district in the northeastern United States during a 15-week time frame. The evaluation attempted to respond to two overarching questions: How can teachers' contributions extend the field about what we know about their teaching practices in CRPs, particularly in large urban school districts? And what can be learned from teachers' contributions in using CRPs that can lead to school improvement? These questions form the basis of the study by examining the connections between urban teachers' perceptions and practices related to an evaluation of a K–12 systematic reading program using a multisensory approach focusing on teaching word structure in English in mainstream classrooms.

Research-Based Programs and Program Evaluation

The present view of reading instruction is highly complex, socially constructed, and politically situated (Pearson, 2003). While other professions see value in using evaluative feedback to guide program planning and evaluation (Schwartz & Baer, 1991), the reading profession tends to be vulnerable to "faddish" practices that may prove flawed or invalid (Moats, 1999). Since NCLB has become an increasingly influential factor contributing to public school districts utilizing CRPs to teach all students (Brenner & Hiebert, 2010), a critical review of such programs requires objective and in-depth analysis (Simmons & Kame'enui, 2003). Since the National Reading Panel (NRP) developed a standard for evaluating the effectiveness of reading instruction mandating that instruction methodology is grounded in scientifically based reading research (NICHD, 2000), the selection and adoption of an effective, research-based CRP has become the hallmark of educational policy makers (Ravitch, 2010). Obviously, the notion to exclude qualitative studies and research methodologies that could be used in instructional programs has had an impact on silencing the voices of reading teachers using such programs (Garan, 2002, 2004).

While there are clearly benefits to examining scientifically based research, rarely does one size fit all students in all situations, and in a number of instances, CRPs "fall short of research recommendations" (Dewitz et al., 2010, p. 308; see also Davis, 2007). In fact, few studies reported have validated any particular reading program at any grade level (Brenner & Hiebert, 2010). In addition, due to the continuing significant disparity in academic achievement among students of various racial, ethnic, and cultural backgrounds, the view that any core program is effective at any given time "remains largely elusive" (Lee, Ajayi, & Richards, 2007, p. 19).

When utilizing program materials such as teacher's manuals, there is a need for careful evaluation because it is unclear which lessons or activities are the most essential to ensuring those students who depend on schools to help them become highly literate are getting appropriate experiences in becoming proficient readers (Brenner & Hiebert, 2010). Moreover, Allington (2012) posits that schools should become more skeptical and informed consumers of materials, methods, and programs particularly related to claims of "research-based" program effectiveness. It has also been argued that in urban districts qualitative methods should be an important part of large-scale program evaluations if program effectiveness is to be determined and understood (Slayton & Llosa, 2005). While challenges exist regarding the use of qualitative research methods, much can be learned to improve program evaluation and generate findings that are meaningful and useful to stakeholders, besides student test data. Thus, when considering program outcomes, the success of a CRP must extend beyond the measures of group achievement test scores (Allington, 2002).

Teacher Input

One dilemma regarding the widespread use of CRPs is what role teachers' play in implementing them. The assumption that any program can have comparable levels of achievement or be equally sustainable with all students, in all situations, all of the time seems unfounded (Allington, 2012). According to Lipson, Mosenthal, Mekkleson, and Russ (2004), research on effective schools discovered that the foundation of successful schools is the teacher. It is also recommended that teachers rely on their knowledge and skills when structuring reading instruction based on CRPs (Dewitz et al., 2009). There is also strong evidence suggesting that teachers be given the responsibility to use their expertise and professional judgment in order to choose readings and offer students the instruction most appropriate to meet their needs (Ravitch, 2003). Unfortunately, what is more likely to occur is that teacher input is largely ignored when their knowledge and skills should be taken into consideration and matter much more than particular curriculum materials, pedagogical approaches, or proven programs. Thus school districts could profit from taking teachers' responsiveness to children's needs into consideration in building their literacy success, regardless of which program is most based on research (Allington, 2002, 2012; Darling-Hammond, 1999).

While there are no fast and easy solutions, Ravitch (2003) recommends that teachers should be trusted more to make their own contributions and decisions in the classroom than to rely on the "highly politicized process that now governs textbook publishing in America" (p. 169). In fact, a more effective solution for reducing the achievement gap might be to reverse the trend that programs must be delivered in the same way and give teachers opportunities to take on a larger role in program design. As outside political and social influences continue to impact what role teachers have in the implementation of CRPs, this chapter describes one urban school district's journey toward improving reading instruction for all students.

CONTRIBUTING AND INFLUENCING FACTORS OF CORE READING PROGRAMS

Public education has become increasingly fixated on raising test scores, suggesting that NCLB has placed an overemphasis on test scores for schools to make "annual yearly progress" in raising student achievement (Primont & Domazlicky, 2006). Unfortunately, teachers are also experiencing the trickle-down effect by spending too much time developing strategies to improve districtwide test scores (Fingon, 2007). Although standardized test scores are useful, they are not very helpful in telling what should be done with poor results or poor student performance (Calhoun, 2004). Thus, as test scores continue to be a top priority, there is the potential for distorting and degrading the meaning and practice of education and becoming a replacement for curriculum and instruction (Ravitch, 2010, p. 111).

One way that states and districts address the press to raise standardized test scores is by implementing CRPs that profess to raise scores when implemented with fidelity. However, when implementing such programs, particularly in large centralized school districts, teacher fidelity issues related to instructional experience and level of training in how to use the program and reading instruction in general tend to surface. *Fidelity,* or the act of conforming, "grounded in empirical research can be described as the extent to which delivery of an intervention or treatment adheres to the program model" (Mowbray, Holter, Teague, & Bybee, 2003, p. 316). Subsequently, if teachers follow the same program regardless of the level of their training, experience, or competence, they often address the instructional needs of the majority of students in a respective school or district, with the underlying assumption that program delivery should work equally well for any child (Duncan-Owens, 2008; Simmons & Kame'enui, 2003). More important, program designers who insist on explicit implementation of program delivery and ignore input from classroom teachers about how they modify their use of program lessons and materials "miss opportunities to make their programs better" and to find out how teachers "develop strategies that are worthy of further investigation" (Duncan-Owens, 2008, p. 16).

However, a more common occurrence seems to be that teachers are caught between exerting their professional knowledge and the need to conform to a mandated CRP (MacGillivray, Lassiter Ardell, Sauceda Curwen, & Palma, 2004). It seems the more experienced teachers perceived the program as too structured and questioned the district's practice of the program's effectiveness to help all students, while the less experienced teachers held a more positive view about the program's structure and felt more confident in following lesson plans. Interestingly, new teachers tend to rely more on scripted lessons and materials in CRPs even if their preservice programs emphasized an improvisational or adaptive approach toward those materials (Dutro, 2010; Valencia, Martin, Place, & Grossman, 2009). Moreover, if teachers dislike the materials or lessons, disagree with the program's philosophy, or are not adequately trained, this ends up creating more subtly "the power of the bottom over the top" (Darling-Hammond, 1999, p. 41). While commercial program developers may acknowledge variability in program implementation, they tend to rely on the assumption that fidelity will either claim or disclaim program effectiveness.

Another concern with implementing CRPs is the notion of "deskilling" in which teachers rely more on the manual to guide their instructional decision making and rely less on their craft (Apple, 1995). This places teachers in a situation that limits their opportunity to use their literacy knowledge and expertise and has a deskilling effect on teachers' practices that can be subtle and ubiquitous in nature (MacGillivray et al., 2004). There is also the concern that CRPs "make no assumptions that the students will grow, that what they learned a week or a month ago is useful in learning the next skill or strategy" (Dewitz et al., 2010, p. 307). Other dangers in using a mandated CRP lie in the fact that the program's goal may take on a narrowing view of literacy in a school district or supplant the overall reading curriculum (Apple, 1995; Ravitch, 2010).

THE STUDY: STONEFIELD SCHOOL DISTRICT

Stonefield School District (SSD—a pseudonym) has over 2,500 students enrolled in seven schools with different grade-level configurations scattered throughout the city. Stonefield's student demographics are typical of most K–12 school districts in the region: Students are predominantly White, native English speaking, with very small percentages of African American, Native American Indian or Alaskan native, Asian, and Hispanic/Latino students speaking a language other than English at home. Most teachers are White and female with an average of 12 years of teaching experience. At the time of the study the standardized reading test scores were slightly above the state mean and scores were beginning to decline.

Wilson Reading System® (WRS), a commercial CRP developed by Barbara Wilson (Wilson, 1998), modeled on the Orton-Gillingham principles and phonological coding research, had been implemented in the SSD for 4 years at the time of the study. Overall, the WRS teaches word structure and language that helps students master decoding and encoding/spelling in a structured sequence using a multisensory approach that is reinforced "verbally, aurally, tactually and visually" (Wilson, 1998). Students learn by hearing sounds; manipulating color-coded sound, syllable, and word cards; performing finger-tapping exercises; writing down spoken words and sentences; reading aloud, repeating what they have read in their own words, and hearing others read it as well. WRS is the first program and one of four program models produced by the company. Research evidence about the program's effectiveness includes mostly literature of testimonials from schools in various regions about their success with the program (Wilson & O'Connor, 1995).

Initially, WRS was implemented by SSD administrators with very little input from K–12 classroom teachers. Prior to program evaluation, it was viewed as the main resource for reading instruction at the primary grades and a major component of the overall reading and language arts curriculum in the district. The administration also perceived that teacher training and fidelity were key components to effective program delivery. Although there were scant numbers of ELLs in the district, no program version that addressed ELLs existed.

The WRS literature recommended students be taught one-on-one or in small groups; however, largely due to financial reasons, the majority of students in the district were taught in whole-class lessons using some component of the program. For example, kindergartners were instructed in the program's phonemic awareness skills, students in Grades 1–2 were instructed in decoding skills, and students in

Grades 3–6 were instructed in the program's spelling (encoding) skills. Students with special needs were instructed mostly one-on-one and Title I students were generally taught in small groups.

I conducted a program evaluation using a mixed methods approach during the CRP's fourth year of implementation. Data were collected and analyzed from all school sites based on interviews, surveys, and classroom observations queried from administrators, principals, classroom and special education teachers, and classroom assistants' feedback regarding their views of the program's overall effectiveness. Classroom observations were conducted followed by teacher interviews. In-house certified program trainers were observed more than once with extensive follow-up interviews. Focus groups were conducted from a selected cross-section of 21 participants including building principals, special educators, classroom teachers, and a small random sampling of students. I also designed and distributed a survey to all reading instructors in the program asking for background information about their teacher training and their overall perceptions and instructional practices related to the effectiveness of the program.

I gathered extensive field notes transcribed from interviews, classroom observations, reading and language arts curriculum committee meetings, and a sampling of grade-level meetings at school sites. Survey responses were also coded and analyzed.

LEARNING FROM TEACHERS' VOICES

Analyzing the many sources of program evaluation data and listening to the voices of teachers helped to elucidate what really was working and not working to improve student learning. While many teachers perceived the program to be working well, data showed where improvement was needed. Perhaps the single most obvious occurrence was reference to the program's name, "Wilson," rather than the subject of reading, by almost all principals, teachers, administrators, staff, and students. Parents also mentioned the program's name during parent-teacher conferences. "Wilson" was also written in teacher's lesson plans and posted on classroom black- and whiteboards.

Interestingly, although classroom teachers in the district were predominantly White and middle class, their perceptions and attitudes about the program were quite diverse. Comments from teachers across the grade levels and school sites about the effectiveness of the program varied based on a number of reasons. For example, special education teachers who taught in the program as a pullout model had mixed views about the program's effectiveness, as expressed in this teacher's comment: "I am not against the program, but why can't we use other resources? I know other resources and strategies that have worked in the past. Some of my LD [learning disabled] students are thriving but what about the rest?" In addition, the lockstep structure of the program was viewed overwhelmingly as both an advantage and disadvantage among the classroom teachers.

As somewhat to be expected, during teachers' daily teaching, they felt pressured to either adhere to or reject scripted lessons, as this third-grade teacher remarked: "Why do we assume one program will serve all students? Some parts of the program work for some kids and not for others. I have this tension every day in my teaching: Do I adapt or comply?"

However, when teachers talked about changes in their practice, some explored additional resources, as this sixth-grade teacher confided: "I know I am not reaching all my students. It is frustrating and discouraging to me because I am required to teach this program and can't use other materials, but I do when I think it is right. Why must it be all or nothing?"

Teachers also voiced social justice concerns and ethical and equity issues about the program's ability to meet students' needs who qualify for reduced or free lunch. These fifth- and sixth-grade teachers' comments from a curriculum committee meeting illustrate this point:

Fifth-grade teacher: How do we help poor and disadvantaged students in my class who only have these resources and no books at home? All they get are these workbooks and that is not acceptable. How do I foster the love of reading for these students?

Sixth-grade teacher: Why are so many resources devoted to this program? It is not proportional to other subject areas.

There were also mixed reactions among the teachers about the overall quality and gaps in students' writing skills and the program's structured spelling (encoding) rules. Teachers expressed frustration over the lack of choice in moving more capable spellers ahead or to the next-grade-level spelling list. As this sixth-grade teacher remarked in a focus group interview, "I feel like we are under the gun to implement the lessons at all costs. If the program is so good, then why don't we have better spellers and writers? There doesn't seem to be much application or evidence from the spelling program to writing."

Comprehension skill building was also part of daily lesson planning; however, based on classroom observations, students mostly learned decoding skills and reading and writing from controlled text. This conversation of a second grader discussing with the researcher what was learned after a lesson exemplifies this point:

> *Researcher:* Do you remember the key words you learned today?
> *Student:* [Smiles and looks at the blackboard and quickly reads] That's easy: stand, stump, and skunk.
> *Researcher:* Very good. Now can you use the words in a sentence?
> *Student:* [Looks down at his desk sitting quietly for a few moments] I'm not sure.
> *Researcher:* That's OK. Can you think of a way to use stand, stump, or skunk—the key words from today's lesson—in a sentence?
> *Student:* [Looks around the classroom before responding] I don't know.
> *Researcher:* Did you write anything down in your notebook today?
> *Student:* [Looks relieved and opens a notebook and quickly reads] The skunk stinks.
> *Researcher:* Great. Now, can come up with another sentence on your own?
> *Student:* [Briefly remains quiet then shrugs shoulders] I don't think we learned that.

Another compelling insight was the noticeable difference in instructional time between various teachers across schools and grade levels using the program. For example, the WRS teacher's manual recommended a quick 2–3-minute review of the previous day's lesson, 45 minutes of instruction with controlled or decodable reading passages, and 15–30 minutes of listening comprehension taught following the lesson or at another time in the day. In most cases, classroom observations showed that daily lessons ranged from as little as 10 minutes a day to as much as 60 minutes a day. However, during follow-up interviews, teachers articulated a rationale for changes in their instruction, as these two third-grade teachers illustrate:

> *Teacher 1*: Sure, I glance at the lesson plans, but I spend very little time on review or following all the steps because most of my students already know the skills. What they really need is more time to practice and apply those skills using real literature, not controlled text.

Teacher 2: I have a lot of struggling readers in my class, and they are showing much more confidence in their reading when I go beyond the recommended lesson time. I see the benefits from the reinforcement of those skills for those students.

In essence, despite teachers' varying perceptions and reluctance to implement the program, their resistance to the program was *not grounded in reluctance to change*; rather, it was based on their concern for their students' literacy success and engagement as learners (Pease-Alvarez & Samway, 2008; Pease-Alvarez, Samway, & Cifka-Herrera, 2010).

Teachers also varied in their practices when using the required program assessments to chart students' progress in decoding and encoding skills. Based on interviews and survey comments, most teachers preferred to use a combination of assessments to guide instruction. Throughout the program evaluation teachers also confided that some students were slipping through the cracks in the program for different reasons. They believed that students who were already reading above grade level would benefit from more challenging lessons and reading materials. Teachers further expressed concern for helping students achieve particularly in schools that had higher percentages of student absenteeism and more severe student behavior issues. Unfortunately, because there were so few ELLs in that district, results of the program's impact for these students was a missed opportunity.

One obvious characteristic of these teachers was their ability to take their "cues from the students they were teaching" (Allington, 2005, p. 462) and seem reasonably confident that their observations were more reliable than the program lessons and materials. It is important to note that in this instance the teachers were able to clearly articulate reasons for modifying their lessons to teach their predominantly White, native English-speaking student population. It is likely teachers using WRS with more culturally and linguistically diverse students would be required to address the ways in which the program afforded access to the curriculum for those students who are less proficient in English. Moreover, providing CRPs have been shown to be less effective for ELLs who are often underserved by such programs (Pease-Alvarez et al., 2010).

What can be learned from the evaluation of the CRP at SSD? First, the evaluation provided evidence and documentation validating teachers' beliefs, perceptions, and instructional practices that sparked new interest in what was really happening regarding reading instruction within the district. More important, it planted the seed and urgency to move forward toward a more common vision and understanding that one program "was not enough" to improve student achievement. Thus, as a number of events unfolded, teachers began taking a larger part in contributing and creating a plan to improve reading instruction within the district.

RETHINKING SCHOOL REFORM

School change does not happen easily; it is dynamic, complex, inter-connected, and requires time and sustained effort (Allington & Walms-ley, 2004). As in SSD's case, the journey to improvement was neither lockstep nor fluid in its approach; and as the district began taking steps to improve the curriculum, a series of events coincided that pushed change in different ways. For example, as the district's standardized reading tests continued to slip, SSD was labeled as a "needs improve-ment" district and a state consultant was assigned. At about the same time, Wilson publishers developed a new program option, entitled *Fundations*, designed specifically for primary grades and whole-class instruction to reduce reading and spelling failure.

Meanwhile, the district began writing a new comprehensive 4-year (K–12) Literacy Development Plan (LDP), which included (1) the original Wilson Program; (2) the new Wilson model, *Fundations*; (3) the *Four Blocks Literacy Framework* (Cunningham, 1998; Cunning-ham, Hall, & Defee, 1991) that focuses on guided reading, self-selected reading, writing, and "working with words"; and (4) another reading program by Houghton-Mifflin. In addition, more professional devel-opment and program training for newly hired teachers was planned because of a high turnover of teachers due to teacher retirement in-centives (information based on a telephone conversation with SSD administrator in Student Support Services on January 29, 2010, and a telephone interview on February 2, 2010; and email correspondence on February 25, 2010 from the new SSD assistant superintendent).

The first year of the reform process comprised the organizing of a group of literacy teacher-leaders (K–12) with assistance from the state consultant to develop staff awareness and receptivity to the district's new LDP. It was bottom-up, more inclusive, and designed to look at the strengths as well as gaps of the current WRS and curriculum while seeking ways to enhance reading instruction and preparing staff for use of other reading programs for general use, with application look-ing different at each school site. The LDP also incorporated some of the state Department of Education's recommended strategies for read-ing instruction:

- Helping students make connections with what they know
- Analyzing structure or figuring out how text is organized
- Exploring inferences
- Thinking between the lines when reading
- Determining important ideas and themes

The LDP was considered a framework for teaching guided by educational, philosophical, and research-based principles. It was designed to be phased in and first piloted at the elementary schools, then employed at the middle school, and later implemented at the high school. The LDP also included an intervention model for Title I/Special Education students focused on literacy. Funding was also provided in the school district budget for teachers, offering paid opportunities for training based on their needs.

PRINCIPLES OF PRACTICE USING CORE READING PROGRAMS

As school districts continue to implement CRPs and raise the level of awareness within the community about such programs, they may run the risk and the likelihood that the program becomes the entire reading and language arts curriculum. Based on a combination of factors and timely events, changes within the SSD had to originate from the teachers and be supported by a broad consensus in order to be successful (Carrigg, Honey, & Thorpe, 2005). Clearly, without input and feedback from all participants, the risk of a program being rejected, misunderstood, or undermined increases (Calhoun, 2004). In fact, through collaborative K–12 schoolwide efforts, rather than replacing one core program for another, the district developed a broader, more comprehensive approach to reading instruction. The district designed a new LDP and framework that incorporated best teaching practices supported by elements of the existing WRS program as well as the newly adopted reading programs for teachers to use as tools to meet students' needs at *each* school site. More important, as teachers became more involved with support from the state consultant, which was not historically practiced in the district, they worked in positive ways and the district slowly transformed from a top-down approach to one that was more inclusive. Furthermore, the school district continues to assess and revise a more localized curriculum to find ways to improve reading instruction for students at all school sites.

The teachers' stories of their experiences with the implementation of a CRP at SSD and the subsequent changes that occurred offer some insight about how to approach the use of CRPs within the current instructional context. Given the focus of the current literature related to effective reading instruction for all students and the fact that CRPs continue to command presence in the field of reading, the following principles of practice for CRP are offered:

1. Reverse the trajectory of the rising influence of commercial program developers in the decision-making process of reading instruction and curricula issues.
2. Consider students' background knowledge, and cultural, linguistic, and socioeconomic differences within the context of the school community when planning curriculum.
3. Consider how the content of core reading programs needs to be critically analyzed as they have become the source and increasing focus in federal and state school reform efforts (Brenner & Hiebert, 2010).
4. De-emphasize the notion that teacher fidelity or compliance is the major cause for a program's success or failure.
5. Allow teachers voice, choice, and opportunity to use their practical, personal, and theoretical knowledge to inform reading instruction (Duffy-Hester, 1999).
6. Provide teachers with access to professional development that is grounded in student work (Carrigg et al., 2005).
7. Respect the commonsense notion that students differ as much as teachers differ and that teacher's knowledge and experience goes beyond the framework of reform (Allington, 2012; Carrigg et al., 2005).

CONCLUSION

During a time of political influences and schools closely monitoring teachers' decisions and instructional practices, this study taps teachers' voices and emphasizes the importance and critical need of their contributions that can lead in positive ways to improve reading instruction for all students. Thus it is not *which* reading program or emphasis is right, but *when* and *for whom* the program can be validated (Alexander & Fox, 2004, Pearson & Kamil, 2010). As the field of reading continues to be influenced by others, Erickson (1991) points out that "how to organize schools genuinely for diversity in literacy, treating multidimensionality as a resource rather than a liability and providing various ways to climb high, is a challenge we continue to face as educators and citizens" (p. x). Irvine (2003) also cautions that if teachers treat all students the same and ignore their ethnic identities and cultural beliefs, this most likely means that all students are taught as if they were or should be "middle class and White." Moreover, as classroom teachers and school principals continue to be predominately White, differences between school and home culture tend to result in lower rates of academic achievement for diverse learners (Spring, 2010). Clearly, as there are differences within culturally and linguistically diverse students, these differences should be reflected when planning reading instruction. As schools strive to improve reading instruction for all and as we continue to examine our own personal ideologies, Allington (2001) surmises, "It will still be the teachers who make the difference in children's lives and teachers who will either lead the change, or resist, or stymie it" (p. 148).

REFERENCES

Alexander, P. A., & Fox, E. (2004). A historical perspective on reading research practice. In R. B. Ruddell & N. J. Unrau (Eds.), *Theoretical models and processes of reading* (5th ed., pp. 33–68). Newark, DE: International Reading Association.

Allington, R. L. (2001). *What really matters for struggling readers: Designing research-based programs*. Boston, MA: Longman.

Allington, R. L. (2002). What I've learned about effective reading instruction from a decade of studying exemplary elementary classroom teachers. *Phi Delta Kappan, 83,* 740–747.

Allington, R. L. (2005). Ideology is still trumping evidence. *Phi Delta Kappan, 86,* 462–468.

Allington, R. L. (2012). *What really matters with struggling readers: Designing research-based programs*. Boston, MA: Pearson.

Allington, R. L., & Walmsley, S. A. (Eds.). (2004). *No quick fix: Rethinking literacy programs in American elementary schools*. New York, NY: Teachers College Press and International Reading Association.

Apple, M. W. (1995). *Education and power*. New York, NY: Routledge.

Brenner, D., & Hiebert, E. H. (2010). If I follow the teacher's editions, isn't that enough? Analyzing reading volume in six core reading programs. *The Elementary School Journal, 110*(3), 347–363.

Calhoun, E. (2004). *Using data to assess your reading program*. Alexandria, VA: Association for Supervision and Curriculum Development.

Carrigg, F., Honey, M., & Thorpe, R. (2005). Moving from successful local practice to effective state policy. In C. Dede, J. R., Honan, & L. C. Peters (Eds.), *Scaling up success: Lessons learned from technology-based educational improvement*. San Francisco, CA: Jossey-Bass.

Cunningham, P. M. (1998). Nonability grouped, multilevel instruction: Eight years later. *The Reading Teacher, 51*(8), 652–664.

Cunningham, P. M., Hall, D. P., & Defee, P. M. (1991). Nonability grouped, multilevel instruction: A year in a first grade classroom. *The Reading Teacher, 44*, 566–571.

Darling-Hammond, L. (1999). *Teacher quality and student achievement: A review of state policy evidence*. Seattle: University of Washington, Center for Teaching Policy.

Davis, S. H. (2007). Bridging the gap between research and practice: What's good, what's bad, and how can one be sure? *Phi Delta Kappan, 88*(8), 569–576.

Dewitz, P., Jones, J., & Leahy, S. (2009). Comprehension strategy instruction in core reading programs. *Reading Research Quarterly, 44*(2) 102–126.

Dewitz, P., Leahy, S. B., Jones, J., & Maslin Sullivan, P. M. (2010). Developing comprehension with core reading programs. In P. Dewitz, S. B. Leahy, J. Jones, & P. M. Maslin Sullivan (Eds.), *The essential guide to selecting and using core reading programs* (pp. 281–308). Newark, DE: International Reading Association.

Duffy-Hester, A. M. (1999). Teaching struggling readers in elementary school classrooms: A review of classroom reading programs and principles of instruction. *The Reading Teacher, 52*, 480–495.

Duncan-Owens, D. (2008, May). *Evidentiary sleight of hand: The high stakes of silencing teachers*. Paper presented at the International Congress of Qualitative Inquiry, Urbana-Champaign, IL. Retrieved from http://eric.ed.gov/PDFS/ED501572.pdf

Dutro, E. (2010). What "hard times" means: Mandated curricula, class-privileged assumptions, and the lives of poor children. *Research in the Teaching of English, 44*(3), 255–291.

Erickson, F. (1991). Foreword. In E. H. Hiebert (Ed.), *Literacy for a diverse society: Perspectives, practices, and social policies* (pp. vii–x). New York, NY: Teachers College Press.

Fingon, J. (2007). No test and No Child Left Behind: Urban teachers' perceptions and realities about standardized testing. *The California Reader, 40*(2), 11–19.

Garan, E. M. (2002). *Resisting reading mandates: How to triumph with the truth*. Portsmouth, NH: Heinemann.

Garan, E. M. (2004). *In defense of our children: When politics, profit, and education collide*. Portsmouth, NH: Heinemann.

Irvine, J. (2003). *Educating teachers for diversity: Seeing with a cultural eye*. New York, NY: Teachers College Press.

Lee, S. K., Ajayi, L., & Richards, R. (2007). Teachers' perceptions of the efficacy of the Open Court Program for English proficient and English language learners.

Teacher Education Quarterly, 34(3),19–33.

Lipson, M. Y., Mosenthal, J. H., Mekkelsen, J., & Russ, B. (2004). Building knowledge and fashioning success one school at a time. *The Reading Teacher, 57,* 534–542.

MacGillivray, L., Lassiter Ardell, A., Sauceda Curwen, M., & Palma, J. (2004). Colonized teachers: Examining the implementation of a scripted reading program. *Teaching Education, 15*(2), 131–144.

Moats, L. C. (1999). Where we are: Taking stock of teacher preparation in reading. In *Teaching reading IS rocket science: What expert teachers of reading should know and be able to do* (11–14). Washington, DC: American Federation of Teachers.

Mowbray, C. T., Holter, M. C., Teague, G. B., & Bybee, D. (2003). Fidelity criteria: Development, measurement, and validation. *American Journal of Evaluation, 24,* 315–340.

National Center for Education Statistics (NCES). (2009). NAEP data explorer: National assessment of educational progress 2009 reading assessment. Retrieved from http://nces.ed.gov/nationsreportcard/naepdata/report.aspx

National Center for Education Statistics (NCES). (2011). The nations's report card: Findings in brief reading and mathematics 2011. Retrieved from http://www.nces.ed.gov/nationsreportcard/pdf/main2011/20124559.pdf

National Institute of Child Health and Human Development (NICHD). (2000). *Report of the National Reading Panel: Teaching children to read: An evidence-based assessment of the scientific literature on reading and its implications for reading instruction. Reports for subgroups* (NIH Publication No. 00-4754). Washington, DC: U.S. Government Printing Office.

No Child Left Behind Act of 2001. Pub. L. No. 107-110, 115 Stat. 1425 (2002).

Pearson, P. D. (2003). The role of professional knowledge in reading reform. *Language Arts, 81*(1), 14–15.

Pearson, P. D., & Kamil, M. L. (2010). Transitioning looking back and looking forward. In M. L. Kamil, P. D. Pearson, E. Birr Moje, & P. P. Afflerbach (Eds.), *Handbook of reading research: Vol. IV.* New York, NY: Routledge.

Pease-Alvarez, L., & Samway, K. D. (2008). Negotiating a top-down reading program mandate: The experiences of one school. *Language Arts, 85*(1), 32–41.

Pease-Alvarez, L., Samway, K. D., & Cifka-Herrera, C. (2010). Working within the system: Teachers of English learners negotiating a literacy instruction mandate. *Language Policy, 9*(4), 313–334. doi 10.1007/s10993-010-9180-5

Primont, D., & Domazlicky, B. (2006). Student achievement and efficiency in Missouri schools and the No Child Left Behind Act. *Economics of Education Review, 25*(1), 77–90.

Ravitch, D. (2003). *The language police: How pressure groups restrict what students learn.* New York, NY: Vintage Books.

Ravitch, D. (2010). *The death and life of the great American school system: How testing and choice are undermining education.* New York, NY: Basic Books.

Schwartz, I. S., & Baer, D. M. (1991). Social validity assessments: Is current practice state of the art? *Journal of Applied Behavior Analysis, 24*(2), 189–204.

Simmons, D. C., & Kame'enui, E. J. (2003). *A consumer's guide to evaluating a core reading program grades K–3: A critical elements analysis.* Portland: University of Oregon, College of Education, Institute for the Development of Educational Achievement.

Slayton, J., & Llosa, L. (2005). The use of qualitative methods in large-scale evaluation: Improving the quality of the evaluation and the meaningfulness of the findings. *Teachers College Record, 107*(12), 2543–2565.

Spring, J. (2010). *Deculturalization and the struggles for equality: A brief history of the education of dominated cultures in the United States.* New York, NY: McGraw-Hill.

Valencia, S. W., Martin, S. D., Place, N. A., & Grossman, P. (2009). Complex interactions in student teaching: Lost opportunities. *Journal of Teacher Education, 60*(3), 304–322.

Wilson, B. (1998). *Wilson Reading System instructor manual.* Millbury, MA: Wilson Language Training Corporation.

Wilson, B., & O'Connor, J. R. (1995). Effectiveness of the Wilson Reading System used in public school training. In C. McIntrye & J. Pickering (Eds.)., *Clinical studies of multi-sensory language education.* Salem, OR: International Multi-sensory Structured Language Education Council.

CHAPTER 2

Effective Bilingual Education Pedagogy for Developing Oral Language and Preliteracy Skills in Hispanic Preschoolers

Virginia Gonzalez

Decades of research provide rich evidence supporting cognitive advantages associated with bilingualism such as higher level critical thinking skills (i.e., creativity, flexibility of thinking, enhanced semantic memory and concept formation, and metacognitive and metalinguistic skills) resulting from a variety of symbols learned during cultural and linguistic experiences (Collier & Thomas, 2004; Gonzalez, Yawkey, & Minaya-Rowe, 2006; Rogoff, 1998). Moreover, extensive research makes it clear that effective dual-language instruction uses the cultural and linguistic diversity of students as rich potential to enhance their cognitive, cultural, and social development, resulting in higher academic achievement and lower attrition rates across grade levels (Calderon & Minaya-Rowe, 2003; Gonzalez, 2001; Snow, 1990). Dual-language instruction is critical, especially for young English language learners (ELLs) who are in the process of acquiring Spanish as their primary language (L1) and English as a second language (L2), as well as for developing oral and preliteracy skills as a scaffold for L2 development and as a cognitive tool supporting their learning across content areas (Echevarría, Vogt, & Short, 2007; Gonzalez et al., 2006). However, the literature is rather scarce for the case of young ELLs in need of developing their oral and preliteracy skills in their L1 and in English. Therefore, this chapter attempts to contribute to the discussion on effective pedagogy for preliteracy and oral language skills for preschool ELLs who are at risk because of socioeconomic limitations at home and in the public schools serving them.

A lot of data support the urgency of using effective reading instruction for at-risk children because of socioeconomic factors, such as living in immigrant households below poverty levels. In 2008–09 the poverty rate increased for all children under the age of 18 from 19% to 20.7%, with higher increases among minorities, for example, an increase to 23.2% for Hispanics and 25.3% for Asians (U.S. Census Bureau, 2008). In addition, *Highlights from the Conditions of Education* reports that 20% of all public elementary schools were considered high-poverty schools, with an increase of Hispanic students from 11% to 22% between 1988 and 2008, and with a decrease of White students from 65% to 55% (U.S. Census Bureau, 2010). In particular, Hispanic immigrant children have a relatively high level of at-risk socioeconomic factors with resulting developmental and educational risks, identified as: a family living in the United States for less than 5 years, being foreign born, having parents who are foreign born, having a non-English-speaking household, and having at least one parent who has not finished high school (U.S. Census Bureau, 2008).

Head Start programs—preschool programs created in the 1960s to help "disadvantaged" students who were generally poor and/or minority children who came to school "already behind their peers in the intellectual skills and abilities required for academic achievement" (Haskins, 2004, p. 27)—have been the focus of research that looks at how to ameliorate such gaps. The National Center for Education Statistics (NCES, 2009) explored the impact of at-risk factors, such as poverty and immigration, in students attending Head Start Programs and found that there was great variation in proficiency in various cognitive skills (i.e., language, preliteracy, math, letter identification, and fine motor skills) between children age 2 and 4 who lived in poverty, as compared with those from higher socioeconomic levels. Specifically, 20% of 4-year-olds in poverty were proficient in letter recognition compared to 37% of their peers at above poverty levels, and 45% of 4-year-olds in poverty demonstrated proficiency in numbers and shapes compared with 72% of their peers above poverty levels.

Due to the significant increase in the number of students coming from ELL, immigrant, and below poverty backgrounds in U.S. public schools, there is a need to identify effective pedagogy supporting their oral language and preliteracy skills. Despite the scarce number of preliteracy studies for preschool ELLs, there is strong evidence for academic achievement gains resulting from early experiences with dual-language instruction. Unfortunately, many teachers and administrators either neglect the research-based evidence or hold misconceptions that fostering students' L1 will impede the growth of English oral language and literacy skills (Barnett, Yarosz, Thomas, Jung, & Blanco, 2007; Krashen, 1997). Therefore, these misconceptions and negative attitudes lead educators to become entangled in how best to teach preschool ELLs who are Hispanic immigrants.

Regardless of this political debate, the weight of the evidence shows multiple advantages for using both primary language and second language as tools or methods for instruction and supports the use of dual-language or two-way bilingual programs. The dual-language approach, which integrates native and nonnative speakers of English in the same classroom and offers instruction in both the primary language and English, strives to bring full oral and literacy skills in both L1 and L2, provide all students with equal learning opportunities, and boost academic achievement (Montecel & Cortez, 2002). Moreover, some studies support Cummins's (1994) theory of language interdependence, indicating that a child's L1 proficiency transfers to L2. In addition, Ramirez and Shapiro's (2007) longitudinal study indicated that young Hispanic children's reading fluency skills transferred between languages.

Slavin and Cheung (2005) reviewed experimental studies comparing bilingual and English-only reading programs for young ELLs. Their findings concluded that even though the number of strong data-based studies is small, existing evidence supports paired bilingual strategies teaching reading in L1 and English. Although studies providing data-based evidence for the effectiveness of bilingual strategies for improving reading skills in young immigrant children are limited, they provide specific pedagogical recommendations. Vaughn et al. (2006) support the effectiveness of a systematic oral language and reading intervention for first-grade, Spanish-speaking, at-risk students. In such a program, trained bilingual intervention teachers provide content that addresses various oral language and reading skills (i.e., letter-sound identification, phonological awareness, word attack, passage comprehension, and reading fluency).

Snow, Burns, and Griffin (1998) explored how immigrant students struggle with English literacy and found that effective teachers, who received training in pedagogy for at-risk learners, were able to use their acquired knowledge to problem-solve and effectively adapt their instructional materials and methods to the particular L1 educational needs of vulnerable children. These teachers received support from their schools in the form of resources and facilities (e.g., manageable class sizes and student–teacher ratios, curriculum materials and libraries, and ongoing professional development) that further enabled them to be more effective teachers for immigrant students. Young and Hadaway (2006) recommend that teachers differentiate biliteracy instruction to meet the needs of individual students' diverse proficiency levels and move at-risk young students from initial social to academic language by presenting content topics through thematic instruction. They also recommend specific instructional strategies related to comprehension, vocabulary development, guided reading, puppetry, and dialogue-journal exchanges to facilitate English language and literacy acquisition.

Cardenas-Hagan and Carlson (2007) document the disadvantages of young Hispanic students in mainstream classrooms with low oral and literacy L1 proficiency, placing a need for L1 instruction before learning the L2 or English as a second language (ESL). They recommend that teachers become aware of similarities and differences existing between English and their students' L1 for creating lessons stimulating positive transfer between languages. Research supporting the importance of using L1 instruction also documents the need to provide ELLs with adequate developmental time for transferring L1 to L2 oral and literacy skills, and for L1 and L2 to be used as methods of instruction across content areas and thematic curricula. One way to do so is to provide students with dual-language instruction. Thus dual-language instruction enhances cognition, language, and cultural identities in ELLs and celebrates their diversity as a social and personal asset.

HOW A DUAL-LANGUAGE CLASSROOM BECAME AN OPEN LABORATORY: TEACHERS AS ACTION RESEARCHERS

This chapter describes classroom observations of Hispanic immigrant preschoolers immersed in a dual-language, bilingual, developmental, multiage Head Start preschool program located in a suburban school of a midsize Midwestern city. It further includes the two teachers reflection and observations of their students' language development processes. The classroom observations and teacher reflections illustrate how dual-language instruction connects oral language and preliteracy development in young ELLs who have Spanish as a first language and English as a second language. It also describes the dual-language program as an open laboratory for teachers to engage in action research and concludes with lessons learned and pedagogical implications from the implementation of the dual-language program for young children's oral L1 and L2 and preliteracy skills. All the names of teachers and students used in the study are pseudonyms.

Description of the Program

The context of this dual-language Head Start preschool classroom developed from a partnership between a local university and a school district designed to serve the growing numbers of ELLs in the local area. Head Start, a national program, promotes school readiness and comprehensive child development services to economically disadvantaged children and families, with a special focus on helping preschoolers develop the early reading and math skills needed to be successful in school (U.S. Health and Human Services, n.d.). The emphasis of the preschool curriculum was on oral language and prereading skills such as vocabulary, sound identification, phonological awareness, and verbal and nonverbal concepts through the use of cognitive and metacognitive strategies (Gonzalez et al., 2006). The curriculum was also based on a socioconstructivist perspective with the interaction of internal (i.e., maturation, psychological, and biological factors) and external (i.e., children's socioeconomic status [SES], cultural and social factors, and family settings) developmental and learning processes (Gonzalez, 2009).

The curriculum used a pluralistic approach, celebrating cultural/linguistic diversity as an asset, enriching the development and learning potential of young diverse children. In the classroom, learning was envisioned as a holistic developmental process across cognitive, linguistic, and socioemotional and academic areas (language arts, mathematics, science, and social studies). Both Spanish and English were viewed as conceptual tools for learning (or methods of instruction) that represented sociocultural and socioemotional processes that are important for young children to develop cultural identity, self-concept, and self-esteem necessary for academic achievement. Teachers created a nurturing classroom in which to establish mutual respect of individual and cultural/linguistic differences, and a personal connection with the child (bonding or rapport). They were also trained in these learning principles to act as mentors and role models, and were stimulated to develop moral responsibility and advocacy for supporting at-risk young children's academic achievement and helping children become resilient learners.

The curriculum implemented followed a two-way bilingual Spanish/English approach. Two pedagogical strategies were employed, a thematic approach and a dual-language spiral curriculum, in order to allow children to have continuity and the necessary developmental time to form conceptual connections and transfer of learning across content areas. That is, the curriculum used parallel (but not repetitive) instructional activities and themes in L1 and L2 across content areas. Teachers systematically delivered instruction in either English or Spanish to promote language development during content instruction, but children were able to respond in either their L1 or L2.

Cindy and Adriana both worked in collaboration as teachers in the bilingual preschool classroom and were also taking masters level courses in the ESL program at the local university. I trained both teachers in the socioconstructivist and pluralistic pedagogical principles on which the curriculum was based. Cindy, a White, native-English speaker from the Midwest was in her late 20s and had 5 years of first-grade teaching experience in suburban local public schools. Cindy also knew limited Spanish-as-a-foreign-language, which she was able to use, if necessary, to communicate with her ELLs. Adriana, a native-Spanish speaker in her middle 20s, was an international student from Costa Rica who had just moved to the United States and had worked for 3 years as an English-as-a-foreign-language teacher in preschool settings in her home country. She was also proficient in English as a foreign language.

Eighteen children were enrolled in the dual-language bilingual preschool, 10 of whom had Spanish as their L1 and were identified as ELLs and 8 of whom spoke primarily English and were from mainstream English-speaking backgrounds. A majority of the children in this multiage preschool classroom were female and children's ages ranged from 3–5—five children were 3 years old, seven children were 4 years old, and six children were 5 years old. In addition to language variations, children also exhibited some developmental differences due to variation in chronological age, number of years of schooling, and maturational levels. All children came from low-income backgrounds and qualified for Head Start services. The mainstream English-speaking children, as well as the ELLs, shared some at-risk conditions as identified by the U.S. Census Bureau (2008), such as their parents had not finished high school and the family was living below poverty levels. Seven out of ten Spanish-speaking children had been born in the United States, but because of their age their parents had been living in the United States for less than 5 years, and Spanish was spoken at home.

A video camera was used to record classroom observations in the bilingual preschool setting and observations were collected three times a week throughout the academic year. The video recordings included a representation of all children participating across content areas taught and languages used. Classroom observations were analyzed in a qualitative manner for uncovering topics and themes emerging as lessons learned or patterns from the study. Based on evidence from the video observations the classroom became an open laboratory, which allowed me (as the researcher) and the two classroom teachers to learn and explore. The presence of a researcher and video camera became an ongoing and constant presence in the classroom, allowing children opportunities to interact in a risk-free environment.

Inside the Classroom

In her journal entry Cindy describes the physical preschool setting:

> The classroom is cozy and spacious with everything kept in
> a neat and tidy order. The book area, the manipulative area
> with puzzles, and the kitchen and block areas are organized
> systematically in the outer part of the classroom. A snack table
> (sometimes also used for special activities), a writing table, and a
> sensory table are set up around the corners of the inner part of
> the classroom.

The following is a description of a typical day at the beginning of the school year in the preschool classroom. Cindy prepares name tags for all children written on labels, and as she pronounces the name of a child and shows the name tag, she asks the child if the name belongs to him or her and to place it on the board. This activity continues until all children recognize their names and place their name tags on the board. Next, the children follow Cindy as she goes to the play station and asks children to sit on the floor and form a circle. As she presents another set of name tags to the children, she models name recognition by showing and reading each name tag aloud and asks them to recognize their name when it appears. Diego, Santiago, Rosa, Sean, Susana, and Julia recognize their name tags before Cindy pronounces them. Guillermo, Mariana, Crystal, and Raul also recognize their names and other classmates' name tags when they are displayed. Cindy also involves the children in placing their name tags on blank spaces provided on the board as they sing the lyrics to a song that is already written on the board. Although some children are singing, most ELLs are not participating. The purpose of these beginning activities as transcribed from classroom video observations builds on cognitive strategies to develop letter-sound identification skills in children.

In another activity that uses metacognitive strategies and aims to develop vocabulary and phonological awareness, the children make the sound that identifies the name of the animal Cindy mentions. While she uses common animal names such as *dog, cat, elephant,* and *piggy* the children can hardly manage to make the sounds of the animals, except for *cat.* When the word *elephant* is prompted, only Susana makes the correct sound; and when *pig* is mentioned, only Sean makes the correct sound. Since it is the beginning of the year, this lesson of imitating animal sounds may be difficult for ELLs because they do not know the English words for animals or they may lack prior knowledge about animal sounds.

Next, Adriana takes the children to the writing center. She gives every child a piece of paper and tells them to "write a letter" to somebody they love. Raul decides to write a letter to his parents. He gives the letter to Adriana—a picture composed of two ovals representing the heads of people, two points symbolizing the eyes, and two horizontal lines representing their mouths. The drawing also has two circles below the ovals representing the legs or trunks, and two vertical lines sketching their arms. When Adriana asks Raul some questions in Spanish about his drawings, she writes the story that Raul tells about his picture.

Meanwhile, Rosa has been busy "writing a letter" sitting at the alphabet table copying the letters on her own. She is not satisfied with the way she writes (copies) the letter *X* and erases it and tries to follow the traces of the letter in the alphabet board located on the table using her index finger. When Rosa calls for Adriana's attention, she says, "*Yo puedo escribir la letra 'X'*" (I can write the letter *X*). Then, as Rosa proceeds to copy some words in Spanish that are displayed on the writing table as models for the children, she draws pictures and then a happy face and says, "Good job!" Rosa seems attached to Adriana and calls Adriana "mama." During snack time Adriana holds Rosa's hand and Rosa hugs Adriana while sitting on her lap.

During another part of the day, children choose whether they want to work with Cindy at the painting table or with Adriana at the sandbox. Adriana takes her group of children holding hands to the sandbox and the children get busy finding tokens Adriana has hidden in the sand. Children need to find red colored objects first, then yellow and blue, and so on. The children are busy searching for small objects in the sand and comment in their L1 and L2 on the colors of the objects they find. This activity uses colors as an example of verbal and nonverbal concept formation for the development of vocabulary. Meanwhile, the rest of the children follow Cindy as she shows her fingers and prompts everybody to model what she does at the painting table. As Cindy shows the girls the red paint, Julia begins painting. Cindy continues to model for the children how to use some sponge patterns (while making stars, houses, apples, trees) to stamp papers as she labels the colors by saying, *"Esta es una manzana roja, esta es una estrella amarilla, este es un arbol verde, y esta es una casa azul"* ("This is a red apple, this is a yellow star, this is a green tree, and this is a blue house"). As the children watch with attention and imitate their teacher, Susana says, *"A mi mama le gusta el amarillo"* ("my mother likes the color yellow"), as she looks at Julia painting with yellow. Cindy then asks the children to make a pattern of "three bright yellow stars" and helps them count each star as they press the sponge patterns on their paper; then they do something similar using "five green trees" and so on. The children seem eager to engage in using the paint and other materials. The purpose of this activity uses the intersection of colors and numbers as an example of verbal and nonverbal concept formation for the development of vocabulary.

In addition, these two last activities (painting and sandbox) illustrate how Cindy and Adriana presented parallel (but not repetitive) instructional activities in a spiral curriculum that used both languages as methods of instruction for teaching concepts across content areas and for stimulating oral language and prereading skills. Subsequently, the curriculum was thematic and presented continuity across content areas throughout the school year, allowing developmental time for young children to acquire content and develop their language and preliteracy skills.

Based on these classroom videotapings and observations, we see that Cindy and Adriana provided a student-centered curriculum with a variety of flexible activities using both languages as methods of instruction for the development of oral language and preliteracy skills. Overall, the classroom scenario described reinforces cognitive and metacognitive strategies and aims to help children develop the following: (1) the connection between verbal and nonverbal concepts (between oral language and symbolic representations such as drawings and letters); (2) the understanding of the functional uses of written language; (3) letter-sound identification; and (4) phonological awareness. Each teacher used one language for instruction and served as native language and culture role models resulting in a spiral curriculum across content areas. Thus the preschool classroom was like an open laboratory for the participating teachers, who were learning from their students by providing dual-language opportunities for the children.

LESSONS LEARNED FROM THE DUAL-LANGUAGE CLASSROOM LABORATORY: IMPLICATIONS FOR DEVELOPING ORAL LANGUAGE AND PRELITERACY SKILLS IN YOUNG ELLS

Educators' misconceptions about bilingual education can be dispelled by exposure to research-based evidence and by actually teaching in high-quality dual-language programs. Cindy, also taking a bilingual education seminar, made these comments about her own teaching and learning:

> After taking a bilingual education course, I wonder why we are not using this approach in all schools. With the evidence supporting L1 instruction, it seems ridiculous to ignore the rich possibilities of dual-language instruction. In class, we discussed the economic, political, and philosophical barriers that have prevented bilingual education from entering classrooms across the United States. It seems that what we need most is to endorse diversity in our country. Rather than putting all of our time, money, and energy toward extinguishing the very skills that make ESL students unique, we should use their multilingual/ multicultural characteristics to improve education in schools.
>
> My studies and exposure to the bilingual preschool classroom have made me an advocate for bilingual education and L1 instruction. I have gained a sense of responsibility and compassion for ELLs, and motivation to value their cultural identity and potential.

We can glean a number of lessons from the study presented in this chapter.

Simultaneous Use of L1 and L2 Benefits All Students

In reflecting on the classroom observations of young L1 and L2 learners, we found developmental patterns within the context of social interactions with peers and teachers consistently appeared in the bilingual preschool setting over time. At the beginning of the school year children separated themselves by dominant language, resulting in Spanish-speaking and English-speaking groups, affectionately called "the ducklings" and "the chicks," that followed the Spanish teacher or English teacher. By midyear these groups of children were intermixing and becoming more bilingual in their interactions, with children using a blend of their L1 and their L2 for communicating in the classroom. Children were also using "interlanguage" such as *code switching* (use of L1 and L2 sequentially in different sentences) and *code mixing* (use of L1 and L2 simultaneously within the same sentence). The young ELLs overcame "silence" using "dual-language" communication modes by responding in their L1 when peers and teachers were using their L2. Thus the simultaneous use of L1 and L2 as methods of instruction has a positive effect on the development of oral and preliteracy skills in young ELLs, as well as in young mainstream children.

Assessing Verbal and Nonverbal Cues

Analyzing nonverbal behaviors in the context of some verbal interactions shed light on the L1 and L2 developmental characteristics, students' potential for learning, and learning progress throughout the year. When analyzing classroom videotapings at the beginning of the school year, children hardly uttered a word and did not show fluency in their L1 or L2. However, when observing the children's nonverbal behaviors (communication by sending and receiving visual messages through gestures, touch, body movement, facial expression, and eye contact), we were able to assess young ELLs' overall learning potential more accurately. Thus, by assessing young ELLs' nonverbal behaviors, we were able to observe the development of oral and preliteracy skills in L1 and L2, preventing the possibility of misdiagnosing developmental language delay (or any other special education condition). While at the beginning of the year we could barely hear the children speak their L1 and L2, observations of their nonverbal behaviors showed children flourishing when given the proper classroom environment.

At about the midpoint of the school year we saw an increase in verbal behaviors in the children's emerging oral skills in L1 and L2. This evidence of progress was shown in the form of "chunks" of language learned from peers and teachers. For instance, one of the first English phrases uttered by Rosa (a monolingual Spanish-speaking girl) was "This is mine," in response to Sean's question to her in English, "Can I have this book?" Rosa was able to use an internalized phrase in English, which she had heard numerous times before from her peers in a socially meaningful and appropriate manner to accomplish a social function: to become assertive about her property.

In fact, vocabulary development did not occur as separate words but emerged in common phrases modeled and repeated frequently by teachers in meaningful contexts across content areas and languages.

In another example, Santiago (a monolingual Spanish-speaking boy) developed his L2 oral skills by repeatedly asking the English phrase, "What is this/that?" to his peers about names of various objects during classroom activities and saying their English responses to himself over and over again. Santiago and Rosa exemplify the active role of most children in learning vocabulary through observation and questioning which was a pedagogical strategy modeled by teachers across lessons. Thus it seems critical that teachers pay equal attention to verbal and nonverbal behaviors when assessing and instructing young ELLs' language development, especially during the first months of schooling. In other words, empower young children by "teaching them how to learn," or focusing on metacognitive skills, and emphasizing meaning rather than linguistic form or cognitive strategies focused on verbal and nonverbal concept formation.

As the school year progressed, children's verbal interactions with their peers and teachers showed growth. Although most children produced fragmented or incomplete sentences, they were able to speak in meaningful ways to communicate with others. For example, when Diego (a Spanish-speaking boy) was asked by his teacher, "What are you doing?" he responded, "I cooking toast." In another example, Susana (a Spanish-speaking girl), who was working in the writing center stated, "I tracing the circle," and when her teacher asked, "What colors are you using?" she responded, "Orange, red, red, red, mixing color. I like it." In both cases, teachers did not correct children's speech in either their L1 or L2; rather, they modeled and prompted children's informal speech. They also monitored children's conversation and only intervened to interpret unclear communication and to model effective modes of speech and social interactions.

Interestingly, most children attempted to repair their sentences or add some information that was first missing after their teachers' clarifications and language models were presented to them. Thus preschool teachers need to pay attention to meaning, rather than form, especially during the first stages of oral L2 development in young ELLs, as well as to serve as language and social models for their students, and assess more potential for learning rather than amount of information learned.

Peer Modeling to Support Language Development

Exposing L1-English to L1-Spanish young children had a positive outcome, as they both served as peer models for language development and enjoyed becoming bilingual together. In fact, the children's verbal behaviors were developmentally at higher levels in both L1 and L2 when interacting with peers than when interacting with teachers. Also, children's language production level was higher when initiating a conversation rather than when responding to verbal interactions. As some children developed their L1 and L2 at faster rates than their peers, they emerged as translators and helpers for other children who still needed help in communicating with teachers and peers in their L2. Thus children were cooperating and functioning as peer models for each other, using their language strengths to balance out the language needs of their peers.

As action researchers, the teachers and I also observed similarities in the language development characteristics of Hispanic and mainstream children coming from low-SES backgrounds. Both groups of children showed learning potential but also developmental delays in L1 oral skills, mostly due to lack of stimulation for social and academic language. When both groups of children were exposed to a high-quality curriculum, their oral language and preliteracy skills blossomed and transferred positively from L1 to L2. Thus preschool teachers would benefit from integrating ELLs with mainstream children rather than isolating them, using means such as the dual-language curriculum because it provides social exposure to peer models for positive L2 development.

Culturally Competent Teachers

Having a teacher who represented the same ethnic, linguistic, and cultural background of children in the classroom had a positive socioemotional developmental effect. Young children also benefit from developing an affective and friendly relationship with teachers from different ethnic backgrounds who had cultural competence in their L1, using familiar phrases and songs. Children enjoyed identifying with teachers as social models for becoming bilingual, as they became aware that their teachers also could use an L2 for social interaction with monolingual or bilingual individuals. Thus children were eager to become more like their teachers, using both their L1 and L2, including nonverbal behaviors, in various social situations in the classroom. Children witnessed using chunks of L1 and L2 that teachers had repeatedly modeled so that they could use them in new social situations to convey proper meaning. Therefore, teachers who learn or represent the ethnic, linguistic, and cultural backgrounds of their diverse students, and make the effort to learn some chunks of their students' L1 and integrate their diverse characteristics in the curriculum and materials may become more culturally competent educators.

A CONCLUDING THOUGHT

All in all, this chapter demonstrates what can be learned by examining classroom observations of Hispanic immigrant preschoolers immersed in a dual-language Head Start program over time. The bilingual classroom laboratory was successful in supporting the faster L2 development in young ELLs as well as in mainstream children, with the added benefit of the continuous development of their L1. Both groups of children also benefited from positive socioemotional development due to the presence of peer models for becoming bilingual, as well as their identification with their teachers as positive models for the use of L1 and L2. Moreover, as preschool teachers Cindy and Adriana developed a student-centered curriculum with meaningful and flexible activities, using both languages as methods of instruction, student learning also benefited from direct exposure to positive transfer as a result of the use of L1 and L2 instruction for developing oral and preliteracy skills.

REFERENCES

Barnett, S., Yarosz, D., Thomas, J., Jung, K., & Blanco, D. (2007). Two-way and monolingual English immersion in preschool education: An experimental comparison. *Early Childhood Research Quarterly, 22*(3), 277–293.

Calderon, M. E., & Minaya-Rowe, L. (2003). Moving toward two-way bilingual programs. In M. E. Calderon and L. Minaya-Rowe (Eds.), *Designing and implementing two-way bilingual programs: A step-by-step guide for administrators, teachers, and parents* (pp. 3–21). Thousand Oaks, CA: Corwin Press.

Cardenas-Hagan, E., & Carlson, C. (2007). The cross-linguistic transfer of early literacy skills: The role of initial L1 and L2 skills and language of instruction. *Language, Speech, and Hearing Services in Schools, 38*, 249–259.

Collier, V. P., & Thomas, T. P. (2004). The astounding effectiveness of dual language education for all. *NABE Journal of Research & Practice, 2*, 1–20.

Cummins, J. (1994). Primary language instruction and the education of language minority students. In C. F. Leyba (Ed.), *Schooling and language minority students: A theoretical framework.* Los Angeles: California State University, Evaluation, Dissemination and Assessment Center.

Echevarria, J., Vogt, M., & Short, D. (2007). *Making content comprehensible for English learners: The SIOP Model* (3rd ed.). Boston, MA: Pearson.

Gonzalez, V. (2001). The role of socioeconomic and sociocultural factors in language-minority children's development: An ecological research view. *Bilingual Research Journal, 25*(1, 2), 1–30.

Gonzalez, V. (2009). *Young children, diverse learners: Celebrating diversity in early childhood.* Thousand Oaks, CA: Corwin Press.

Gonzalez, V., Yawkey, T. D., & Minaya-Rowe, L. (2006). *English-as-a-Second-Language (ESL) teaching and learning: Classroom applications for pre-K through 12th grade students' academic achievement and development.* Boston, MA: Allyn & Bacon.

Haskins, R. (2004). Competing visions. *Education Next, 4*(1), 26–33.

Krashen, S. (1997, January). *Why bilingual education?* ERIC Digest (ERIC No. ED403101). Retrieved from http://www.usc.edu/dept/education/CMMR/FullText/WhyBilingualEdKrashen.pdf

Montecel, M. R., & Cortez, J. D. (2002). Successful bilingual education programs: Development and the dissemination of criteria to identify promising and exemplary practices in bilingual education at the national level. *Bilingual Research Journal, 26*(1), 1–20.

National Center for Education Statistics (NCES). (2009). *The Condition of Education: Preprimary study.* Retrieved from http://nces.ed.gov/programs/coe/indicator_epr.asp

Ramirez, R., & Shapiro, E. (2007). Cross-language relationship between Spanish and English oral reading fluency among Spanish-speaking English language learners in bilingual education classrooms. *Psychology in the Schools, 44*(8), 795–806.

Rogoff, B. (1998). Cognition as a collaborative process. In D. Kuhn & R. S. Siegler (Eds.), *Cognition, language, and perceptual development* (pp. 679–744). New York,NY: Wiley.

Slavin, R. E., & Cheung, A. (2005). A synthesis of research on language of reading instruction for ELLs. *Review of Educational Research, 75*(2), 247–284.

Snow, C. E. (1990). Rationales for native language instruction in the education of language minority children: Evidence from research. In A. Padilla, H. Fairchild, & C. Valadez (Eds.), *Bilingual education: Issues and strategies* (pp. 60–74). Newbury Park, CA: Sage.

Snow, C. E., Burns, M. S., & Griffin, P. (1998). *Preventing reading difficulties in young children: Recommendations from the Committee on the Prevention of Reading Difficulties in Young Children.* Washington, DC: National Academies Press.

U.S. Census Bureau. (2008). *Risk factors areas: Data from the 2007 American community survey 1-year estimates.* Washington, DC: Author.

U.S. Census Bureau. (2010). *Highlights from the Condition of Education 2010.* Retrieved from www.nces.ed.gov/programs/coe/press/highlights2.asp

U.S. Health and Human Services. (n.d). *Office of Head Start.* Retrieved from http://www.acf.hhs.gov/programs/ohs/

Vaughn, S., Linan-Thompson, S., Mathes, P., Cirino, P., Carlson, C., Pollard-Durodola, S. D., Cardenas-Hagan, E., & Francis, D. (2006). Effectiveness of Spanish instruction for first-grade ELLs at-risk for reading difficulties. *Journal of Learning Disabilities, 39*(1), 56–73.

Young, T. A., & Hadaway, N. (Eds.). (2006). *Supporting the biliteracy development of English learners: Increasing success in all classrooms.* Newark, DE: International Reading Association.

CHAPTER 3

"You Gotta Say What's in the Book in Your Own Words"

Creating Spaces for Second Language Literacy Development in an Urban Multiage Classroom

Sharon H. Ulanoff, Ambika G. Raj, Diane Brantley, and Susan Courtney, with Richard Rogers

Much has been written about how children do and don't learn to read and write, including those who come to school speaking a language other than English. Children come to school with a great deal of knowledge about literacy, for example, sound-symbol relationships and text directionality. Often children's prior experiences with language and print can have a significant impact on their emerging reading success (Liebling, 2001). For English language learners, oral language proficiency has been shown to have a positive impact on reading proficiency (August, 2003; August & Shanahan, 2006).

Differences in school literacy achievement levels between culturally diverse students and their mainstream counterparts have long been documented (Au, 1998, 2002). This is especially true when factors such as poverty and language background are considered within the context of urban schools (Compton-Lilly, 2004). Not only did the number of English language learners in schools shift from 9% in 1979 to 21% in 2008 (Aud et al., 2010), more than 60% of ELLs in grades K–12 come from poor families (August & Shanahan, 2006). Poverty has been shown to have a negative impact on academic success, with poor students receiving lower scores on measures of reading proficiency (August & Shanahan, 2006).

Given the fact that teachers throughout the United States work in increasingly diverse classrooms, it is important to explore teacher-related programmatic responses to the teaching of reading that can help teachers better meet the needs of all students. Allington and Mc-Gill-Franzen (2004) argue that the most important factor in teaching reading is the quality of classroom reading instruction independent of the materials used for such instruction. RAND Reading Study Group (2002) agrees, stating that "good instruction is the most powerful means of promoting the development of proficient comprehenders and preventing reading comprehension problems" (p. xvii). Within such a view of instruction the curriculum also needs to be challenging and offer equal opportunity for diverse learners (Shepard, 2004). The question becomes, then, what instructional conditions promote success in reading and writing, especially for ELLs?

Initial literacy instruction may vary from class to class or district to district, but there appear to be some constants, such as arguments that support the importance of the development of automatic decoding skills in order to promote reading success (Adams, 1990; Konold, Juel, & McKinnon, 1999; NICHD, 2000) as well as those that support reading instruction that is situated in a more holistic understanding of the words in context (Goodman, 1986). These issues related to effective initial literacy instruction become even more compelling when examined within the context of their application to ELLs.

In this chapter we ask the following research question: How does the multiage experience impact second language (L2) literacy development for ELLs in one urban elementary classroom? A growing body of research describes benefits and challenges for multiage education (Aina, 2001; Anderson & Pavan, 1993; Chase & Doan, 1996; Edwards, Blaise, & Hammer, 2009; Gnadinger, 2008; R. Gutierrez & Slavin, 1992; Lauer, 2000; Lloyd, 1999; Mack, 2008). These benefits include the notion of choice (Doan & Chase, 1994), the view of the classroom as a learning community with a focus on "child-centeredness" and constructivist, inquiry-based pedagogy (Harste, 2001), and the ability to meet the needs of both low- and high-achieving students within an alternative context to the traditional graded classroom (Song, Spradlin, & Plucker, 2009). Challenges to successful multiage classrooms include a lack of institutional support (Miller, 1995), a lack of parental support, and inadequate teacher preparedness (Song et al., 2009).

Multiage classrooms can provide opportunities for language and literacy learning for ELLs within the framework of a learning community. Gutierrez, Baquedano-Lopez, Alvarez, and Chiu (1999) argue that language and literacy learning is inextricably embedded in the social context and/or the structures in place that either support or impede learning. When such structures motivate students to engage in reading and make meaning of text, they increasingly support student success (Guthrie, 2001). Within multiage contexts, children engage in a variety of multifaceted tasks that promote language and literacy development (Gnadinger, 2008). The lessons in which these tasks occur provide opportunities for students to use language in meaningful ways to make sense of classroom activities. Some of these opportunities involve the use and appropriation of different kinds of classroom talk (Ulanoff, Gopalakrishnan, Brantley, & Courtney, 2010; Ulanoff & Quiocho, 2004), or discourse (Gee, 1996; Hicks, 1995), in addition to engaging in meaningful conversations around text (Santori, 2011).

As students become more adept at talking during classroom activities, such as listening to stories or participating in whole-class or small-group discussions, they increase their repertoire of language and knowledge practice (Hicks, 1995), appropriating school discourse and demonstrating success in school tasks, including literacy development (Gillies & Khan, 2008; Nystrand, 2006; Ulanoff & Quiocho, 2004). Hicks (1996) suggests that "discourse is a central means through which new understandings are negotiated among participants" (p. 105). Gee (1996) further argues that students use language as a social tool to help them accomplish interactional tasks in order to making meaning of content and internalize learning.

In addition to providing a variety of opportunities for teacher and student interactions, multiage classrooms may have positive implications for L2 literacy learning and instruction for ELLs. Peer teaching and cross-age tutoring have been shown to be highly effective approaches for ELLs because these practices allow students to utilize language in a social and academic context, thereby enhancing overall language skills while maintaining a high degree of age-appropriate content area instruction (Johnson, 1988). These practices further allow for students to interact in multiple ways related to classroom discourse; and as students become more socialized to classroom interaction and behavioral norms, they come to internalize school language practices (Heath, 1983). These school language practices generally include specific ways in which students and teachers talk to each other (Ulanoff & Quiocho, 2004) during lessons and other classroom activities.

This chapter explores the nature of classroom instruction in one multiage classroom in Los Angeles to look for ways in which the two classroom teachers create spaces for language and literacy learning (Gutierrez, 2008) for 40 students, most of whom are ELLs. It is through instructional practices that allow students to bring their prior knowledge and different ways of knowing that the teachers provide opportunities for students to engage in a community of learners.

A GLIMPSE INTO THE MULTIAGE CLASSROOM

Walking into this multiage classroom in La Nieta School (a pseudonym) means walking into the hustle and bustle of approximately 40 students, two teachers, and a variety of other adults as they go about their daily work. Children are seated on the floor or at a few tables on the outer perimeter of the classroom, clustered in pairs, small groups, or sometimes large groups working with one of the teachers or other adults. La Nieta Elementary School—a pre-K–5, multitrack, year-round school situated in the greater Los Angeles area—has a population of approximately 1,200 students,consisting of 96% Hispanic/Latino, 3% African American, and less than 1% each of all other ethnicities. Seventy-nine percent of the students are identified as ELLs and 98% of the students receive free or reduced-price lunch.

The school neighborhood consists of both single-family homes and multiple-family dwellings that were built in the 1950s and 1960s, and the school itself has an active relationship with a local university and supports a parent center on campus. Many of its teachers are bilingual and others hold certification to teach ELLs. La Nieta School, which is part of a large unified public school district, uses a basal reader as mandated by the districtwide adoption of the text; however, the teachers in the multiage classroom are given some freedom to modify and adapt the curriculum as long as attention is paid to the scope and sequence of the mandated texts.

As we enter the classroom, we are drawn to a pair of students sitting on the rug with a book spread out between them. Roberto, age 5, and Luis, age 7, participate in numerous literacy activities throughout the school day, and the following exchange is a small glimpse into one of those events, where Luis takes on the role of teacher as he works with Roberto to read through a new text.

Luis: Oh . . . .
Roberto: Start reading it.
Luis: But, but that wasn't in the book. That was just in the
        pictures. You gotta say [what's in the book] in your own
        words what kinda cake was it. What kinda cake it was, you
        got to tell her . . .

All around the room students are engaged in reading together, writing in their journals, working on the computer, and doing other activities in pairs and triads. The only thing that distinguishes the two teachers, Susan and Richard, from the rest is their size—they are adults among kindergarten, first-, and second-grade students. The room feels more like a playroom set up for discovery activities than a traditional classroom in a traditional school district. The ambience is one of companionship, where even the youngest students have responsibilities, which they perform with confidence. But this is not a typical classroom in La Nieta School. The only multiage classroom in the school, it is housed in a self-contained trailer away from the main school buildings. Inside the trailer there are two adjacent classrooms with a door between them that is open at all times, providing a fluid space. Both teachers, who are bilingually certified, use English as the language of instruction at all times, although Spanish is used as needed to clarify concepts or explain unknown vocabulary. Students generally enter the class in kindergarten and exit at the end of second grade. The classroom teachers had worked together in the multiage classroom for 9 years when the study began.

THE INQUIRY

This inquiry spans 3 academic years (which start in July in this year-round school) and uses an ethnographic approach to explore the ways in which the two teachers in this multiage classroom create spaces for literacy development for all of the students in their classroom, especially the ELLs. At the beginning of the first year of the study there were 36 students (29 ELLs and 7 English-only learners) in the classroom community, 22 boys and 14 girls ranging in age from 4 to 8 years of age. Although the students were technically divided between the two teachers into separate rosters, they functioned as one multiage classroom. These demographics changed in the second and third years of data collection when the teachers received 10 first-grade students from another class that closed. Other minor changes occurred when students moved or when new kindergarten students replaced second graders who went on to third grade.

The inquiry was conducted by a multidisciplinary research team that consisted of three researchers from a local university who served as "nonparticipant observers" in the classroom and by one of the two classroom teachers who acted as a "complete participant" (Gold, 1958; Junker, 1960). Data collection began the first week of class in July 2003 in order to examine and document the construction of practice, classroom setup, and teacher and student interactions. Each week, one or more of the three researchers observed in the classroom for a minimum of 2 hours during the first year of the study. Second-year data collection included twice-monthly observations by at least one of the three researchers, and during the third year each researcher visited occasionally to support data gathered during the first 2 years. All observations, which were video- and audiotaped, lasted a minimum of 2 hours. The classroom teachers were present during all observations. Sociocultural theory, which posits that learning takes place within the framework of social interactions (Jennings & Di, 1996; Vygotsky, 1962; Wertsch, 1984), formed the foundation for the study. Activity theory as a means of analyzing the specific actions that took place in the classroom (Engestrom & Middleton, 1996; Leont'ev, 1978; Rogoff, 1990) provided a lens through which to view and understand the interactions and activities occurring within the learning situation.

Multiple data sources were collected during each observation to develop an in-depth understanding of the culture of the multiage classroom. Ethnographic field notes (Emerson, Fretz, & Shaw, 1995), audio and video recordings of classroom practices during blocks of time that were devoted to reading and writing, family journals, math workshop, calendar, and so on, and student artifacts were collected during each observation. The researchers met with the teachers formally and informally throughout the study, as a means of conducting member checks during the data collection and analysis phases of the study, allowing the researchers to clarify and/or modify any interpretations and conclusions they had drawn and to help the researchers understand the teachers' stories. These meetings were also audio- and videotaped and the data served to enrich and triangulate the findings (Merriam, 1995). Data were analyzed, categorized, compared, and contrasted using a methodology that seeks to "elicit meaning from the data" (LeCompte & Preissle, 1993, p. 235) and construct categories or cultural domains (Spradley, 1980).

CREATING SPACES FOR SECOND LANGUAGE LITERACY DEVELOPMENT

Several overarching themes that serve as the context for language and literacy development in this multiage classroom emerged from the data (see Table 3.1). These themes describe the structures in place that impact the classroom community and the framework that supports

TABLE 3.1. Critical Elements of the Multiage Classroom

Themes	Examples
Community and respect	All community members have a voice in decision making in the classroom.
	Parents play an integral role in the classroom community.
Communication	Notes go home in the language of the parents.
	Open-door policy exists for parents and other family members.
	School uses student's L1 for communication as needed.
Print-rich environment	Student work is highlighted throughout the classroom.
	Library provides easy access to books and other materials.
	Written charts and notes appear all over the room.
High expectations in a safe environment	Students take on leadership roles—apply for and receive jobs.
	Students are responsible for one another in addition to their own work.
Integrated curriculum	English language development and literacy instruction are integrated into other content areas.
	Reading and writing take place in all content areas.

language and literacy acquisition and development. Susan and Richard focus on allowing students to make meaning of school activities, learn and use literacy in meaningful ways, and connect new learning to prior knowledge. The themes that emerged from the data serve to highlight the critical elements of this multiage classroom.

Community and Respect

There is an instructional focus on community, respect, and belonging that begins with the first day of school. Returning students are expected to be role models for newcomers. There is an equal level of respect for all community members; everyone is important rather than no one is important. For example, during one lesson Susan was listening to a student when Richard walked over to ask her a question. Susan looked at Richard and said, "Excuse me, but I am listening to Viviana now so I can't talk to you at this moment," indicating to students their equal status. This incident is only one example. Similar events take place throughout the school day.

Furthermore, the class members consistently demonstrate respect and value for the diversity of languages, ethnicities, and cultures in the classroom. While the class is taught in English only, all languages are valued and respected. Both teachers are bilingual (English/Spanish) as are most of the students. Both students and teachers offer primary language (L1) support throughout the day. It is not uncommon to hear Susan or Richard say to a student, *"Dime en español,"* when they sense that the student knows the concept but is searching for the label in English. Students also use Spanish among themselves when scaffolding instruction for each other.

Collaboration is encouraged and modeled throughout the day. Students often work in pairs or small groups to accomplish school tasks. As students and teachers collaborate, learners of all ages are able to work within their personal zones of proximal development (Vygotsky, 1934/1978). Students receive immediate feedback and have multiple opportunities to engage in various conditions for learning (Cambourne, 2002). Students take responsibility for learning as they work together to understand, apply, and make approximations for new concepts and skills across the curriculum, all the while developing language and literacy skills necessary for L2 acquisition. As students collaborate, they receive comprehensible input (Krashen, 1994, 2005) and their strengths are highlighted, which affects their self-esteem and achievement. There is also collaboration with family members, who are considered part of the classroom community and are evident in the classroom throughout the school day, as well as before and after school. There is a notion of shared ownership of and participation in the community.

Communication

There is a high degree of communication between the two teachers; it is almost as if they function as one person. Throughout the day, decisions are made by both teachers as to the direction they will take both procedurally and instructionally, with continual efforts to take both perspectives into account. It is always a discussion rather than a mandate. There are differences, however, in the ways they interact with students; for example, Susan is referred to by her first name, while Richard is called Mr. Rogers, acknowledging each individual teacher's preference.

FIGURE 3.1. Classroom Environment

Parents are also kept in the information loop. Not only do notes go home related to class activities, but parents, teachers, and students consistently communicate with one another. The teachers' bilingual skills come into play here, but it is more the communicative context that serves to open the lines of communication. The notion that parents, teachers, and students talk to each other is a cornerstone of the program that has been strengthened and fostered over 3 years.

Print-Rich Environment

The classroom provides the students with a print-rich environment that emerges during the first few weeks of every school year as the classroom community works to construct a literate environment. Student work is prominently displayed and changes throughout the school year (see Figure 3.1). There is a large library with both fiction and nonfiction texts in English and Spanish at a variety of reading levels. There are charts and lists with important classroom information displayed throughout the room.

High Expectations in a Safe Environment

Both teachers and students have high expectations for the quality of work students are expected to complete in class. These expectations include behaviors that students exhibit in class and on the playground. Everyone looks out for one another and there is no hesitation to step in and refocus a student as needed. The students are expected to be responsible for the group rather than just for themselves. These expectations are consistently communicated to students and parents.

Another way that students take risks while connecting literacy, practical skills, and meaningful learning can be seen in the "writers' office," where students fill out applications for classroom jobs, such as line leader, calendar monitor, or homework checker. The applications request practical information such as the student's address, phone number, and date of birth, as well as a section that asks the applicants to list their qualifications for the position. The prospective employees (the students) must go through an interview process, and just as in the real world, they are rewarded for a job well done and can also be fired for not following through with the responsibilities required of the job. Typically, two students hold one position, an older second- or third-year student (6 or 7 years old) and a first-year student (4 or 5 years old). In doing so, the more experienced student mentors a younger student who will eventually take a leadership role in the classroom.

Susan and Richard create an atmosphere where students are called upon to actively engage in all classroom activities. Support is provided through the use of modeling, questioning, and prompting, as well as L1 support as needed. Students help each other with tasks during instruction and other classroom activities and also feel safe asking for assistance from both teachers. This serves to establish an environment in which the students feel comfortable taking risks with their learning. Moreover, parents feel safe to participate in classroom activities and to bring their concerns to the teachers.

Integrated Curriculum

Music, literature, writing, and science are integrated into weekly lessons. Both teachers spend time activating the students' background knowledge to find out what they already know when introducing a new concept, unit, or book. Thus students are able to use what they know about the world in their L1 to make sense of new knowledge in their L2—meaning from one language therefore transfers to the students' new language (Cummins, 2000).

Beginning in kindergarten, reading and writing are presented across the curriculum with a focus on strategy instruction, such as how to use graphic organizers, word walls, or predictions, to help students make sense of text. This is especially interesting given that teachers in this public school are required to follow the district's ad-opted scripted reading program that is heavily based on phonics and phonemic awareness instruction. Both teachers have adapted their use of the basal materials by infusing minilessons on relevant strate-gies in order to present a thematic approach that embeds their instruc-tion in context and supports the students.

Throughout the year students develop inquiry projects based on questions they have about certain subjects or topics. These projects integrate science and social studies concepts while requiring the stu-dents to conduct research. Students use their developing L2 literacy skills and strategies to research answers to their questions. This often requires reading periodicals and nonfiction texts, using the Internet, conducting experiments, and taking notes while preparing and cre-ating presentations. Presentations take many forms, such as three-dimensional art projects and murals, singing and playing musical instruments, dramatic interpretations, and publishing books.

Rather than engaging the students in decontexualized tasks throughout the day, the teachers emphasize metacognitive awareness and students are asked to verbalize the strategies they have or will use when reading, writing, or approaching a specific task. They repeat directions that the teachers give them before they begin reading, for example, "Read the paragraph silently to yourself. Think about the story we read yesterday and see if this paragraph reminds you of that story." In doing so, students make connections that help them assimi-late new information and facilitate learning that makes sense to them and is fun (Piaget, 1952).

SPACES IDENTIFIED

By design, Susan and Richard create spaces for literacy development by constructing a safe classroom environment where students are free to take risks with their learning and become valuable members of the classroom community. It is common to see English-dominant students trying to speak Spanish with ELLs who take on the role of experts in this area. Students who are just beginning to acquire their second language (L2) interact with students who have acquired more basic and academic language (Cummins, 1994, 2005), offering the beginning ELLs a variety of models to listen to and the opportunities to engage in conversation and dialogue in their emerging L2 (English). All student approximations with language are valued and celebrated, creating a mutually beneficial relationship and safe zone for all students to practice and play with language. The themes that emerged from the data illuminated several types of spaces that are evident in the multiage classroom. We will discuss *environmental spaces* and *linguistic spaces* here.

Environmental Spaces: Creating the Classroom Community

Each year Susan and Richard negotiate a common theme with the students, which becomes the platform for building community within the classroom. This theme drives the instructional focus for that year and the classroom environment, which takes the shape, form, and look of an ecosystem constructed as the school year progresses. The backbone for the environment remains the same and includes the books, the carpet areas for large-group instruction and meetings, the furniture that one would expect to see in a home rather than a classroom (such as rocking chairs, couches, cushions, and benches), and the various nooks and crannies for individuals, pairs, and small groups to work collaboratively. The instructional perspective is based on common pedagogical beliefs that both teachers hold about learning theory, including Cambourne's (2002) Conditions of Learning, and the social contexts for learning supported by Vygotsky (1934/1978), Piaget (1952), and Bruner (1986).

As the classroom habitat is constructed, students conduct inquiry projects and presentations that will contribute to the actual fauna and flora of the current setting. These projects support the varied ways children develop and represent their understanding and learning (Gardner, 1993) and provide opportunities for L2 language and literacy development. For example, when studying the rain forest, students conducted research about various Amazonian wildlife forms, which became part of the ever-growing classroom habitat. The daily class schedule requires the students to set monthly, weekly, and daily goals for themselves with regard to what they want to study, read, and write. For example, students were asked to compile a list of the

100 words they would be able to read in 100 days. Students began the list during the first week of school and kept a record of their growing vocabulary lists throughout the year. Once they reached 100 words, they began their second set of words to learn to read. They also kept a monthly reading reflection where they described the types of things they liked to read and kept a record of the total number of books read during the month. This reflection, along with the daily reading log, became a yearlong record of the students' emerging reading habits.

In the multiage classroom, every child is capable of making decisions and shares in the responsibility for learning. Minilessons are held on various skills and strategies the students will need in order to choose appropriate books and tools that will help them in their inquiries. While the students research information for their projects, Susan and Richard confer with and hold small-group strategy lessons with targeted students who need specific lessons based on assessments the teachers integrate into their daily routine.

These classroom themes serve as the context for instruction, allowing students to make connections to prior knowledge and also to create new background knowledge about learning the specific topic. The content is then linked to literacy instruction through a variety of literature and activities, such as book talks, read alouds, reading responses, and journals. Students actively engage in the themes. For example, the year they studied the African Savannah, the students took a virtual trip to the African Savannah. The next year they created a rain forest in the classroom (refer to Figure 3.1).

Linguistic Spaces: Creating Opportunities for Talk

The teachers use language in ways that not only communicate, but also teach L2 language and usage. Susan and Richard use targeted procedural and instructional talk aimed at both classroom management and also instruction and work: "teacher talk." They further teach students to use both procedural and instructional talk during classroom activities through "self-talk," aimed at helping students internalize instructional and behavioral procedures. Teachers use a "questioning mode" to impel students to search for answers to instructional and procedural questions.

Throughout the day Susan and Richard use teacher talk in ways that both describe and model classroom procedures. *Teacher talk* has been defined as the specific adjustments that language teachers make to the form and function of their speech in order to communicate with students acquiring language (Sharpe, 2008; Xu, 2010). We further use the term to describe the ways in which Susan and Richard used language to teach students specific strategies, procedures, and behaviors in the classroom within the context of both formal and informal conversations (Hayes & Matusov, 2005). The first few days of the school year are spent on group building and teaching appropriate classroom behaviors to the new students in class. Newcomers are paired with returning students in newcomer/role model pairs and returning students are expected to take on expert roles in acclimating the new students to the classroom culture.

For example, during one observation in the third week of the school year in July 2004, all students were engaged in writing letters to pen pals. The students were working independently while the two teachers circulated around the room giving assistance as needed. In addition to getting help from the teachers, students were relying on each other for help. Even the kindergartners were working independently and writing, although Susan stated that in the beginning of the school year "you can pick out a few of the 'new' students." After a few weeks it is almost impossible to tell who is new to the class that school year.

Both teachers teach and use what they call "self-talk" with the students. This consists of specific phrases that help students know how to behave in the classroom. The teachers model the specific behaviors that they expect of students, and then students create "posters" of these statements, which are then placed throughout the room (see Figure 3.2). Furthermore, teachers and students engage in choral self-talk chants at the beginning of the year to help the students learn the classroom procedures. At first they chant with prompting, but after a while students are asked to repeat the self-talk without prompts.

Susan and Richard also use a variety of methods to ensure that students know how to participate in the classroom. Students use a "daily plan" that organizes their school day much like a day planner used by adults. The specific activities in which they are expected to participate are listed in a class-developed four-point rubric posted in the room, and students must evaluate how well they complete their work on a daily basis (see Figure 3.3). Students are expected to work with partners and also to use self-talk.

Susan and Richard are active participants in instruction, modeling behavior and "thinking aloud" as they engage in classroom activities. They both use questioning to get students to think about classroom activities and model L2 vocabulary usage throughout instruction, pos-

FIGURE 3.2. Student "Self-Talk" Poster

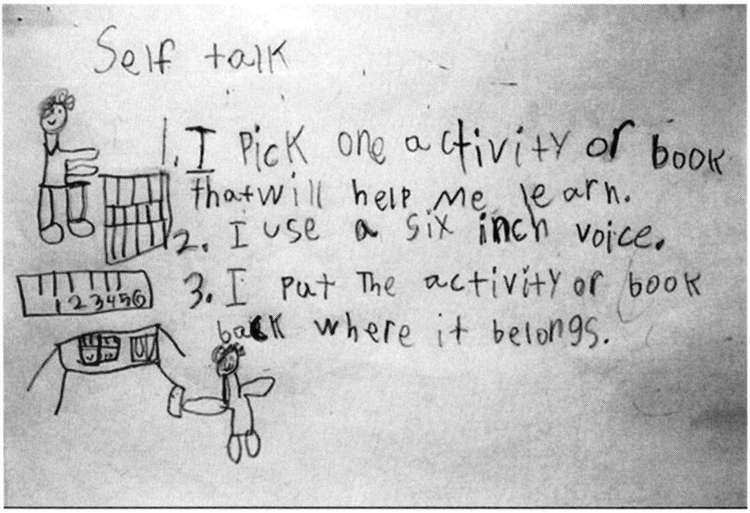

ing critical questions and often responding with questions that hold students accountable for learning. It is through the use of questions that both teachers guide the students to take ownership of their learning as well as develop a sense of collaboration within the classroom community. This is evident during reading instruction when Susan reads aloud to the class. She consistently checks for understanding and then models the use of new vocabulary, embedding it in the context of the story being read and making sure that ELLs have access to the text. During lessons, Susan models the expectations she has for student behavior, including turn-taking behavior during lessons and discussions. She often tells students, "Show me; don't tell me." The expert role models are also quite adept at appropriately scaffolding the procedural information for the newcomers.

Despite the fact that all instruction takes place in English, the L2 of most students in this class, students use Spanish when they are working together, especially when they were giving instructions to other students. While at first glance this appears to be little more than translating to support one another and clarify instructions, further examination reveals that the students are operating within their comfort zone, using their L1 for communication. It may also be used as a means of forming more personal relationships with other students in the class.

FIGURE 3.3. A Portion of the Daily Plan Rubric

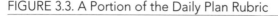

Our Daily Plan Rubric

4 = Wow!

- I read my book or at least three chapters and logged it in.
- I read with my partner for at least 20 minutes. My partner initialed my log.
- I wrote neatly, checked my spelling and punctuation, and published my work.
- I finished and met my goal.
- I planned my day and followed my plan.
- I was responsible and followed all the steps for self talk.

However, students consistently appropriate the self-talk used by Susan and Richard in the classroom, but with subtle differences, demonstrating the students' abilities to internalize and modify self-talk to meet their communication needs. For example, one student, exasperated at another student for critiquing his work, yelled, "I did it to the best of my ability, ok, huh?" This is slightly different from a question that Susan might ask (Did you do it to the best of your ability?). Students also appropriate teacher talk when they take on leadership roles in the classroom. It was not uncommon to hear Ivonne, who is currently in the job of the classroom leader, say, "We have about one minute left," or "Hey, raise your hand if you know," much as Susan or Richard might say to the class.

THINKING ABOUT THE DIFFERENT SPACES

This chapter documents how a multiage classroom supports the L2 language and literacy acquisition and development of ELLs in one public school in California. The goal of the 3-year study was to make visible those processes that allow ELLs to not only acquire English, but also excel within the educational system, thus allowing them access to the same educational opportunities as their English-speaking peers. The findings indicate that the teachers developed a classroom learning community that promoted respect for one another based on a high degree of communication between community members. At all times teachers and students maintained high academic and behavioral expectations for one another, generally holding one another accountable for fulfilling these standards. Additionally, instruction was provided in a safe, well-maintained, print-rich environment through the use of a high-interest, literature-rich, integrated curriculum. Students were encouraged to take ownership of their learning, beginning within the first few weeks of kindergarten and increasing as they progressed into higher grade levels.

Over the course of the study Susan and Richard consistently engaged their students in the learning process through the use of higher level questions, student-led lessons and activities, group-building strategies, and genuine dialogue. As students appropriated and adapted teacher self-talk into conversations with their peers, it became apparent that they had internalized much of the teacher self-talk modeled and reinforced over time because they were able to alter the language and use it within different academic situations. Through this process, the students were able to create *their own* self-talk. This is an important finding as it shows that ELLs in the early stages of L2 acquisition are able to understand and appropriate complex English language concepts through the use of scaffolded instruction by skilled teachers when it is reinforced across a period of 2–3 years. These findings support the notion that students of diverse linguistic, economic, and cultural backgrounds succeed when they have opportunities to engage in "a continuum of teaching strategies that involves them in motivating, meaningful reading [and learning] experiences" (Au, 2002, p. 409). These experiences should take place within a safe learning environment with high academic expectations and a high degree of support from parents, teachers, and students.

IMPLICATIONS FOR L2 LITERACY ACQUISITION

Children who come to school speaking a language other than English face challenges related to the language of instruction and restrictions associated with how and what is taught in reading (Moustafa & Land, 2002; Pease-Alvarez, Samway, & Cifka-Herrera, 2010). Presently the majority of ELLs in California are being taught to read in English, most often through the use of scripted programs that do not always focus on the construction of meaning and come with rigid pacing plans that are often enforced throughout the school. Teachers, in many instances, feel coerced to stick to such scripts and pacing plans, even when they feel that there are better ways to promote literacy success (Pease-Alvarez et al., 2010).

The teachers in the multiage classroom described here demonstrate the ways in which their community of learners supported L2 acquisition and student success. Advocates of multiage education believe that the presence of older and younger children allows them to engage in meaningful literacy activities by encouraging collaboration and promoting a climate of "expected cooperation" (Katz, Evangelou, & Hartman, 1991, p. 10). It is during these activities that children learn to problem-solve and negotiate alternative responses to the problems they encounter, thereby scaffolding each other's learning experiences (Gillies & Khan, 2008; Pontecorvo & Zucchermaglio, 1990; Rojas-Drummond & Zapata, 2004). It is during these interactions that meaningful literacy learning takes place. Multiage classrooms can serve as a context to foster such learning experiences and therefore provide effective spaces to support ELLs' literacy development as they acquire English.

REFERENCES

Adams, M. J. (1990). *Beginning to read: Thinking and learning about print.* Cambridge, MA: MIT Press.

Aina, O. E. (2001). Maximizing learning in early childhood multiage classrooms: Child, teacher, and parent perceptions. *Early Childhood Education Journal, 28*(4), 219–224.

Allington, R. L., & McGill-Franzen, A. (2004). Looking back, looking forward: A conversation about teaching reading in the 21st century. In R. B. Ruddell & N. J. Unrau (Eds.), *Theoretical models and processes of reading* (5th ed., pp. 5–32). Newark, DE: International Reading Association.

Anderson, R. H., & Pavan, B. N. (1993). *Nongradedness: Helping it to happen.* Lancaster, PA: Technomic.

Au, K. H. (1998). Social constructivism and the school literacy learning of students of diverse backgrounds. *Journal of Literacy Research, 30*(2), 297–319.

Au, K. H. (2002). Multicultural factors and the effective instruction of students of diverse backgrounds. In A. E. Farstrup & S. J. Samuels (Eds.), *What research has to say about reading instruction* (pp. 392–413). Newark, DE: International Reading Association.

Aud, S., Hussar, W., Planty, M., Snyder, T., Bianco, K., Fox, M., Drake, L. (2010). *The condition of education 2010* (NCES 2010-028). Washington, DC: National Center for Education Statistics, Institute of Education Sciences, U.S. Department of Education. Retrieved from http://nces.ed.gov/pubs2010/2010028.pdf

August, D. (2003). *Supporting the development of English literacy in English language learners: Key issues and promising practices* (Rep. No. 61). Baltimore, MD: Johns Hopkins University, Center for Research on the Education of Students Placed At Risk. Retrieved from www.csos.jhu.edu/crespar/techReports/Report61. pdf

August, D., & Shanahan, T. (2006). Developing literacy in second-language learners*: Report of the National Literacy Panel on language-minority children and youth.* Mahwah, NJ: Lawrence Erlbaum.

Bruner, J. (1986). *Actual minds, possible worlds.* Cambridge, MA: Harvard University Press.

Cambourne, B. (2002). The conditions of learning: Is learning natural? *The Reading Teacher, 55*(8), 758–762.

Chase, P., & Doan, J. (1996). *Choosing to learn: Ownership and responsibility in a primary multi-age classroom.* Portsmouth, NH: Heinemann.

Compton-Lilly, C. (2004). *Confronting racism, poverty, and power: Classroom strategies to change the world.* Portsmouth, NH: Heinemann.

Cummins, J. (1994). Primary language instruction and the education of language minority students. In C. F. Leyba (Ed.), *Schooling and language minority students: A theoretical framework.* Los Angeles, CA: California State University, Evaluation, Dissemination and Assessment Center.

Cummins, J. (2000). *Language, power, and pedagogy: Bilingual children in the crossfire.* Buffalo, NY: Multilingual Matters.

Cummins, J. (2005). Teaching the language of academic success: A framework for school-based language policies. In C. F. Leyba (Ed.). *Schooling and language minority students: A theoretico-practico framework* (3rd ed., pp. 3–32). Los Angeles: LBD Publishers.

Doan, J., & Chase, P. (1994). *Full Circle: A New Look at Multiage Education*. Portsmouth, NH: Heinemann.

Edwards, S., Blaise, M., & Hammer, M. (2009). Beyond developmentalism? Early childhood teachers' understandings of multi-age grouping in early childhood education and care. *Australian Journal of Early Childhood Education, 34*(4), 55–63.

Emerson, R., Fretz, R., & Shaw, L. (1995). *Writing ethnographic fieldnotes*. Chicago, IL: University of Chicago Press.

Engestrom, Y., & Middleton, D. (1996). *Cognition and communication at work*. New York, NY: Cambridge University Press.

Gardner, H. (1993). *Creating minds*. New York, NY: Basic Books.

Gee, J. P. (1996). Vygotsky and current debates in education: Some dilemmas as afterthoughts to discourse, learning and schooling. In D. Hicks (Ed.), *Discourse, learning and schooling* (pp. 269–282). New York, NY: Cambridge University Press.

Gillies, R. M., & Khan, A. (2008). The effects of teacher discourse on students' discourse, problem-solving and reasoning during cooperative learning. *International Journal of Educational Research, 47*, 323–340.

Gnadinger, C. M. (2008). Peer-mediated instruction: Assisted performance in the primary classroom. *Teachers and Teaching: Theory and Practice, 14*(2), 129–142.

Gold, R. (1958). Roles in sociological field observation. *Social Forces, 36*, 217–223.

Goodman, K. (1986). *What's whole about whole language?* Portsmouth, NH: Heinemann.

Guthrie, J. T. (2001). Contexts for engagement and motivation in reading. *Reading Online, 4*(8). Retrieved from http://www.readingonline.org/articles/art_index.asp?HREF=/articles/handbook/guthrie/index.html

Gutierrez, K. D. (2008). Developing a sociocritical literacy in the third space. *Reading Research Quarterly, (43)*2, 148–164.

Gutierrez, K. D., Baquedano-Lopez, P., Alvarez, H. H., & Chiu, M. M. (1999). Building a culture of collaboration through hybrid language practices. *Theory Into Practice, 38*(2), 87–93.

Gutierrez, R., & Slavin, R. E. (1992). Achievement effects of nongraded elementary schools: A best evidence synthesis. *Review of Educational Research, 62*(4), 333–376.

Harste, J. (2001). What education as inquiry is and isn't. In S. Boran & B. Comber (Eds.), *Critiquing whole language and classroom inquiry* (pp. 1–17). Urbana, IL: NCTE.

Hayes, R., & Matusov, E. (2005). Designing for dialogue in place of teacher talk and student silence. *Culture and Psychology, 11*(3), 339–357.

Heath, S. B. (1983). *Ways with words: Language, life, and work in communities and classrooms*. New York, NY: Cambridge University Press.

Hicks, D. (1995). Discourse, learning and teaching. *Review of Research in Education, 21,* 49–95.

Hicks, D. (1996). Contextual inquiries: A discourse-oriented study of classroom learning. In D. Hicks (Ed.), *Discourse, learning and schooling.* New York, NY: Cambridge University Press.

Jennings, C., & Di, X. (1996). Collaborative learning and thinking: The Vygotskian approach. In L. Dixon Krause (Ed.), *Vygotsky in the classroom: Mediated literacy instruction and assessment* (pp. 77–92). White Plains, NY: Longman.

Johnson, D. M. (1988). ESL children as teachers: A social view of second language. *Language Arts, 65*(2), 154–164.

Junker, B. (1960). *Field work.* Chicago, IL: University of Chicago Press.

Katz, L., Evangelou, D., & Hartman, J. (1991). *The case for mixed-age grouping in early education.* Washington, DC: National Association for the Education of Young Children.

Konold, T. R., Juel, C. & McKinnon, M. (1999). *Building an integrated model of early literacy acquisition.* Ann Arbor, MI: CIERA. Retrieved from www.ciera.org.

Krashen, S. D. (1994). Bilingual education and second language acquisition theory. In C. F. Leyba (Ed.), *Schooling and language minority students: A theoretical framework.* Los Angeles: California State University, Evaluation, Dissemination and Assessment Center.

Krashen, S. D. (2005). Bilingual education and second language acquisition theory. In C. F. Leyba (Ed.), *Schooling and language minority students: A theoretico-practical framework* (3rd ed., pp. 3–32). Los Angeles, CA: LBD Publishers.

Lauer, P. A. (2000). *Instructional practices and implementation issues in multi-age classrooms.* Aurora, CO: Mid-continent Research for Education and Learning.

LeCompte, M., & Preissle, J. (1993). *Ethnography and qualitative design in educational research.* San Diego, CA: Academic Press.

Leont'ev, A. N. (1978). *Activity, consciousness, personality.* Englewood Cliffs, NJ: Prentice Hall.

Liebling, C. R. (2001). Beginning reading: Learning print-to-sound correspondence. In S. Brody, (Ed.). *Teaching reading: Language, letters and thought* (2nd ed.). Milford, NH: LARC Publishing.

Lloyd, L. (1999). Multi-age classes and high ability students. *Review of Educational Research, 69*(2), 187–212.

Mack, J. (2008). Continuous progress schools see the "whole child." *Education, 129*(2), 324–326.

Merriam, S. (1995). *Qualitative research and case study applications in education.* San Francisco, CA: Jossey-Bass.

Miller, W. (1995). Are multi-age grouping practices a missing link in the educational reform debate? *NASSP Bulletin, 79*(568), 27–32.

Moustafa, M., & Land, R. (2002). The reading achievement of economically disadvantaged children in urban schools using Open Court vs. comparably disadvantaged children in urban schools using non-scripted programs. *2002 yearbook of the urban learning, teaching and research special interest group.* Los Angeles: California State University.

NICHD. (2000). *Report of the national reading panel.* Washington, DC: US Government Printing Office. Retrieved from http://www.nichd.nih.gov/publications/nrp/report.cfm

Nystrand, M. (2006). Research on the role of classroom discourse as it affects reading comprehension. *Research in the Teaching of English, 40*(4), 392–412.

Pease-Alvarez, L., Samway, K. D., & Cifka-Herrera, C. (2010). Working within the system: Teachers of English learners negotiating a literacy instruction mandate. *Language Policy, 9*, 313–334. doi 10.1007/s10993-010-9180-5

Piaget, J. (1952). *The language and thought of the child.* London, UK: Routledge & Kegan Paul.

Pontecorvo, C., & Zucchermaglio, C. (1990). A passage to literacy: Learning in a social context. In Y. Goodman (Ed.), *How children construct literacy: Piagetian perspectives* (pp. 59–98). Newark, DE: International Reading Association.

RAND Reading Study Group. (2002). *Reading for understanding: Toward an R&D program in reading comprehension.* Santa Monica, CA: RAND. Retrieved from http://www.rand.org/pubs/monograph_reports/2005/MR1465.pdf

Rogoff, B. (1990). *Apprenticeship in thinking: Cognitive development in social context.* San Francisco: Jossey-Bass.

Rojas-Drummond, S., & Zapata, M. (2004). Exploratory talk, argumentation and reasoning in Mexican primary school children. *Language and Education, 18*, 539–557.

Santori, D. (2011). "Search for the answers" or "Talk about the story"?: School-based literacy participation structures. *Language Arts, 88*(3), 198–207.

Sharpe, T. (2008). How can teacher talk support learning? *Linguistics and Education, 19*, 132–148.

Shepard, L. A. (2004). The role of assessment in a learning culture. In R. B. Ruddell and N. J.Unrau (Eds.), *Theoretical models and processes of reading* (5th ed., pp. 1614–1635). Newark, DE: International Reading Association.

Song, R., Spradlin, T. E., & Plucker, J. A. (2009). The advantages and disadvantages of multiage classrooms in the era of NCLB accountability. *Education Policy Brief* (Center for Evaluation and Education Policy), 7(1), 1–3, 6–7.

Spradley, J. (1980). *Participant observation.* Orlando, FL: Harcourt, Brace & Jovanovich.

Ulanoff, S. H., Gopalakrishnan, A., Brantley, D., & Courtney, S. (with Rogers, R.). (2010). Examining second language literacy development in an urban multi-age classroom. In N. P. Gallavan (Ed.), *Annual editions: Multicultural education* (15th ed., pp. 149–154). New York, NY: McGraw-Hill.

Ulanoff, S. H., & Quiocho, A. (2004). Exploring teacher and student talk during kindergarten inquiry lessons. *International Journal of Early Childhood Education, 10*, 75–89.

Vygotsky, L. (1962). *Thought and language.* Cambridge, MA: MIT Press.

Vygotsky, L. S. (1978) *Mind in society: The development of higher psychological processes* (M. Cole, V. John-Steiner, S. Scribner, & E. Souberman, Eds. & Trans.). Cambridge, MA: Harvard University Press. (Original work published 1934)

Wertsch, J. V. (1984). *Culture, communication and cognition.* New York, NY: Cambridge University Press.

Xu, X. (2010). Analysis of teacher talk on the basis of relevance theory. *Canadian Social Science 6*(3), 45–50.

CHAPTER 4

The Young Writers Group

Increasing Struggling Elementary
Students' Literacy Achievement
Through Dialogue and Technology

Jodene Kersten Morrell

> *We, after all, are concerned with helping students write themselves and their interests into the teeming world of language.*
>
> Charles Bazerman (2004, p. 64)

While No Child Left Behind (NCLB; U.S. Dept. of Education, 2002) is highly controversial, most stakeholders can agree with two principles of the act: (1) Raising achievement for all students is the ultimate goal; and (2) disaggregating data measures progress and is critical for working to narrow achievement gaps (Education Trust, 2003). Yet, since its enactment in 2002, the literacy achievement of certain groups remains consistently lower than that of their peers, particularly English language learners (ELLs), African Americans and Latinos, children from low-income backgrounds, and males (NCES, 2007a; 2007b). While NCLB is successful in pressuring educators and students to demonstrate accountability, it allows little room for diversity of practice and curricula for educators to successfully meet the needs of all students. It also ignores the fact that most textbooks are written for the average, monolingual English speaker (Apthorp, Bedrova, Dean, & Florian, 2001) and after the fourth grade are often written 2 or more years above the average students' reading ability (Allington, 2002).

This chapter discusses a context in which the marginalized and lowest achieving students are neither ELLs nor students with special needs. In fact, compared to the majority of their peers who are ELLs, these students scored half as well on the state standardized test and were not considered fluent readers and writers in the middle of their third-grade year; however, they expressed a strong desire to do well in school and improve their academic achievement. Their parents and grandparents were involved in their education and frustrated with their children's declining achievement and increasingly negative attitudes toward school. The majority of the participants in this study shared one or more characteristics often associated with lower literacy achievement: male, low-income, and Latino. The slight variation among the participants was gender as two of the eight students who participated in the program for the majority of the 16-month program were females. However, both were identified as low-income and both were living with one parent, either a mother or father, and their siblings.

All but one of the participants in this study had attended the research site, Edison Elementary (pseudonym), since kindergarten. All but one student, Jesus, who had come to Edison 6 months earlier from Mexico, had attended summer school at least once. All participants were encouraged by their third-grade teachers to attend summer school between their third- and fourth-grade years. The literacy instruction during the regular school day was not producing the expected growth in literacy achievement and their teachers rightly considered the children far below grade level. While their oral language development would be considered at grade level except for Jesus, who was just beginning to learn English, participants' reading and writing abilities were far below those of their peers. Therefore, a different approach to teaching literacy was needed, which led me to develop the Young Writers Group (YWG), an after-school literacy laboratory.

EDISON ELEMENTARY AND THE YOUNG WRITERS GROUP

Through a federally funded Teacher Quality Enhancement grant, my university created professional development schools with local districts and I volunteered to serve as the faculty university liaison for Edison Elementary. In my role, I placed approximately 100 university students in elementary-grade classes to complete their early fieldwork for the credential program, served as the student teacher supervisor, and worked closely with the Edison staff to identify ways our university could support them and their K–6 students.

Edison, a diverse elementary school, is described as "on the urban fringe of a large city" (U.S. Department of Education, 2011) in Los

Angeles County. Seventy-eight percent of the students speak a first language other than English and 25% are categorized as ELLs (20% Mandarin, Cantonese, and Korean; 5% Spanish). However, based on results from annual state standardized tests, Asian students score nearly twice as high as Hispanic/Latino students. They also score higher than the White students. Based on findings of ELLs' performance on state tests, we would assume the Asian students' scores would be lower due to the higher percentage of ELLs, but this is not the case.

Edison offers after-school programs such as musical productions, student council, math and music programs, art, tutoring, and Gifted and Talented Education (GATE). All teachers have full credentials and are NCLB compliant. In 2007 Edison received the National Blue Ribbon Award and was a Distinguished School in 2000 and 2006. The overall Academic Performance Index (API) score was 910. Students in grades 2 to 4 learn to play the piano keyboard and students in grades 4 to 6 may participate in band or orchestra. Students in grades 4 to 6 may also compete in track and field. Based on this information, Edison appears to be an outstanding school. However, when data are disaggregated, as required by NCLB, we see that not all students are thriving (see Table 4.1).

Based on conversations with the Edison staff and university student teachers, in-class observations of student teachers, and staff meeting discussions, it was evident that a small population of students was struggling and needed additional support. In January 2007 I asked third-grade teachers to select the students who were struggling the most and send their parents a letter I had written in Spanish and English, inviting their children to join the YWG. The group began with eight students meeting after school, continued through summer school, swelled to 20 students through fall, then moved into the fourth-grade classroom for the winter, and ended in April 2008.

During our initial meeting I introduced myself as Mrs. Morrell and invited students to introduce themselves. Nick, a White native-English speaker, introduced himself as "I can't read." Like Nick, the other students were shy and hesitant to read and write, often stating that they didn't know how. By third grade, they were keenly aware of their identities as readers and writers. They understood what it meant to be a strong reader and writer within the classroom context, what Wenger (1998) would describe as a "community of practice" with its own language, routines, and social interactions. Within the school context, they viewed themselves as nonreaders and nonwriters, which was not entirely true. Most were reading one to two grade levels below but would not be considered nonreaders or nonwriters.

TABLE 4.1. Student Population and Achievement at Edison Elementary (2008)

	Enrollment	ELLs	California Standards Test: Proficient in English Language Arts*
Asian	463	20%	86%
Hispanic/ Latino	125	5%	46%
White	22		56%
Filipino	18		95%
Total	628		

*California Standards Test: High-stakes state test administered yearly for Grades 2–8; statistics represent students at or above the proficient level.

Nevertheless, they felt alienated and knew they were not performing as well as peers or as well as they should for a third grader.

The YWG was a 16-month program, but this chapter focuses on the summer session, which included seven of the original eight students who continued in the YWG through fourth grade. I chose to focus on this 5-week block of time, rather than the one-hour after-school program during the school year, because it most closely mirrors the typical school day. Two to three days each week, the Young Writers (YWs) left their summer-school class to work in our YWG classroom, a portable building at the back of the school that also served as a classroom and staff meeting room during the school year.

The primary goal of the YWG was to increase literacy achievement by focusing on standards; yet what made it unique and effective was how it differed from the type of instruction given during the regular school day. In their classrooms the students typically experienced whole-group instruction and reliance on the basal reading program. In the YWG we experimented with more authentic ways of learning with the support of dialogue and technology. Initially, the students mentioned that they preferred to read informational text and poetry; however, they unanimously voted, by a show of hands, to focus on narrative reading and writing for the summer session. As students wrote narratives, we did an interactive read-aloud of the Great Illustrated Classics version of *The Invisible Man* (Wells, 2002), initially chosen from one of the book talks I had selected to introduce to the students to entice them to read. They also selected three other Great Illustrated Classics books: *The Adventures of Sherlock Holmes* (Doyle, 1993), *Dracula* (Stoker, 2005), and *The Three Musketeers* (Dumas, 2002). Students then modeled elements of their writing on the novel. I focused on the third-grade standards with which the students continued to struggle along with the fourth-grade standards that fit with the goals of our summer session (see Table 4.2).

As in the YWG from January to June, I encouraged students to discuss their ideas, ask questions about the texts, and engage one another in dialogue. These had become important characteristics of our "community of practice" (Wenger, 1998) and allowed me to identify areas where they continued to struggle, such as comprehending text, making connections, and increasing their vocabulary. Out of the discussions, particularly from questioning, I could focus instruction on gaps in understanding. In the summer, technology became an important tool for increasing the quality and quantity of the participants' writing, especially when coupled with dialogue. The remainder of this chapter discusses the critical role of dialogue and technology as mediating tools (Vygotsky, 1934/1978) for helping participants to develop as readers and writers.

Dialogue and Writing

Lantolf (2000) explains how, "while separate, thinking and speaking are tightly interrelated in a dialectic unity in which publicly derived speech completes privately initiated thought" (p. 7). Essentially, thinking and speaking should be explained in relation to one another since each informs the other. Sociocultural theory, originated by Vygotsky, is extremely helpful for considering the connection between learning and dialogue in the classroom. Aukerman, Belfatti, and Santori (2008) suggest that:

> Teaching children in ways that encourage them to engage with each other's voices may foster *agency* (action that follows from the belief that one's ideas matter for how others think and proceed), *the ability to evaluate and contest truth claims* (rather than accepting ideas as a predetermined given from elsewhere), and *a capacity to listen carefully* (identifying and responding to how others see the world). (p. 341; italics in the original)

Aukerman et al. found that encouraging children to engage in dialogue can foster learning, help students think critically, and increase confidence. Indeed, with the Young Writers, dialogue was vital for producing higher quality and quantity of writing because it made the task easier and they could rely on each other for support.

TABLE 4.2. Third- and Fourth-Grade Standards Addressed During Summer Session

	Standards: Grade 3	Standards: Grade 4
Writing strategies	*Evaluation and Revision* Standard 1.4. Revise drafts to improve the coherence and logical progression of ideas by using an established rubric.	*Organization and Focus* Select a focus, an organizational structure, and a point of view based upon purpose, audience, length, and format requirements. *Evaluation and Revision* Standard 1.10. Edit and revise selected drafts to improve coherence and progression by adding, deleting, consolidating, and rearranging text.
Writing applications: genre characteristics	Standard 2.1. Write narratives: a. Provide a context within which an action takes place. b. Include well-chosen details to develop the plot. c. Provide insight into why the selected incident is memorable. Standard 2.2 Write descriptions that use concrete sensory details to present and support unified impressions of people, places, things, or experiences.	Standard 2.1. Write narratives: a. Relate ideas, observations, or recollections of an event or experience. b. Provide a context to enable the reader to imagine the world of the event or experience. c. Use concrete sensory details. d. Provide insight into why the selected event or experience is memorable.
Written and oral English language conventions	Sentence structure Grammar Capitalization Spelling	Sentence structure Grammar Punctuation Capitalization Spelling

Vygotsky (1934/1978) found that speech plays a critical role in accomplishing tasks, such that "the more complex the action demanded by the situation and the less direct its solution, the greater the importance played by speech in the operation as a whole" (p. 26). For the participants, writing was an extremely complex task and when asked to write quietly and independently the quality and quantity of their writing was far less than when they discussed their ideas prior to and while writing. They often shared complex retellings of events and books and demonstrated in-depth knowledge of real world concepts (e.g., regeneration of lizard tail, reptiles, automobile engines, and sports), but when asked to write about these, they became silent or put down their pencils and stared at their notebooks. When given the opportunity to cowrite and discuss ideas prior to writing, the product was superior to their individual writing. Dialogue allowed them to question text, ask for clarification of word meaning, and listen to one another's ideas, questions, and comments.

The participants routinely selected expository text or poetry from home to share with the group or to read when we visited the school library each week for independent reading; however, in the summer they voted to write narratives. We spent the first week studying the elements of a narrative and creating one together. This process included a great deal of dialogue and a combination of traditional handwriting and technology.

As we cowrote the narrative, I considered their writing tendencies and what hindered their success. Since struggling writers often minimize the importance of planning prior to writing, or as Graham, Harris, and Mason (2005) explain, "They typically start writing with little or no forethought, generating ideas on the fly, as they write" (p. 210), and as a result "struggling writers typically demonstrate little persistence when writing and produce compositions that are relatively brief, incomplete, and of poor quality" (p. 211). Therefore, we spent a significant amount of time prewriting prior to drafting. The YWs often struggled to organize ideas on paper despite having details and complex ideas in their minds that they could orally articulate. Hence I had them discuss and use graphic organizers (visuals used to help students add information as they write) from their language arts program to generate details about characters based on images of people from magazines. We developed a plot line on the whiteboard and participants added and deleted ideas, which was open for discussion and modification as we wrote the narrative. They were also encouraged to include interesting dialogue. As we wrote the collective narrative, we referred to *The Invisible Man* (Wells, 2002) to discuss important narrative elements.

As the YWs discussed and dictated the narrative based on the graphic organizers, I typed their words on my laptop. They gathered around the laptop and marveled as their words appeared while I typed. The following day they each received a hard copy of the narrative, which we edited and revised together, each handwriting on their own copies. They were encouraged to discuss their edits, similar to peer revision. As MacArthur (2007) explains, peer revision "is often recommended as a way to providing student writers with an audience of readers who can respond to their writing, identify strengths and problems, and recommend improvements. Students may learn from serving in roles as both author and editor" (p. 146). Peer revising is also most effective when coupled with instruction based on evaluation criteria or revising strategies, which we employed throughout the writing process.

On the third day, we discussed their suggestions and typed the changes on the laptop. On the fourth and final day of the first week, they received the "published" narrative. The writing process was a combination of traditional handwriting and use of the laptop.

When it was time for students to create their own narratives, they discussed their characters' qualities, plot, setting, and dialogue prior to writing. Using a graphic organizer, they wrote a general beginning, middle, and end and had to discuss it with at least two other participants for clarification. They were very good at asking questions and clarifying ideas, and writing had become a more social and collaborative endeavor than what they experienced in their typical school day. The YWs were excited to share their texts, just as MacArthur (2007) explains, that "peer collaboration is also highly motivating, and it reflects the reality that most writing tasks outside of school are surrounded by rich oral communication" (p. 160). Additionally, in a review of research on peer collaboration, Cho and Schunn (2007) state that researchers found that "peer collaboration is effective in that students working alone are unlikely to detect their own misunderstanding and contradictions in text, to consider audience, but students working collaboratively are better able to avoid these problems" (p. 412).

Over the next 3 weeks, I met with students in pairs or triads to work on their narratives. As they dictated their narratives, based on their graphic organizers, their peers gave feedback. My role was primarily to type as they spoke their narratives. Similar to the process used with creating the group narrative, I typed their words and printed hard copies, which they received the following day to edit and revise by hand. As individual students went through the writing process, they were forced to clarify their ideas and address assumptions about their audience. The author's partner(s) helped the author to analyze his or her writing on multiple levels, from the specific words to the tone of the writing, character development, creativity of plot, and literary devices. Participants experienced the writing process with the support of dialogue to produce clear and engaging narratives.

Technology and Writing

Pritchard and Honeycutt (2007) assert that "today, writers of all ages are familiar with technology. By middle school, students are adept at hand-eye coordination and can easily grasp the more advanced editing/revising capabilities of word processing programs" (p. 34). We also know that the majority of research on technology in the classroom focuses on Internet use, technology as an add-on, and is situated in secondary and professional programs (Brown & Dotson, 2007; Dunlap, 2006). However, approximately 95% of K–12 classrooms in the United States have Internet access, 80% of kindergartners use computers, and over 50% of children younger than nine use the Internet on a regular basis (Barone & Wright, 2008). Based on reviews of research of technology in the classroom, specifically in relation to literacy, the majority of research does not address students in low-income, urban contexts or students' perceptions (see Lankshear & Knobel, 2003; NICHD, 2000). Unlike most available research, the YWG focused on the use of technology to support the writing development of historically marginalized students in elementary school.

Jessica, who struggled the most to produce text by hand, urged me to use the laptop as a tool to write the collective narrative since I could not write their words fast enough on the whiteboard. This same process was used for all YWs to create individual narratives. Since January, Jessica had watched intently as I typed field notes. She also asked to read them, to which I agreed. I soon found that using the laptop made revisions far more appealing to the participants because they did not have to handwrite their narratives and could focus on higher level standards, including clarifying ideas, improving dialogue, focusing on word choice, and improving spelling by seeing the correct spelling of words on the screen.

I found MacArthur's (2007) assertions about computers and struggling writers to be true for the YWs. He states, "Computers are powerful and flexible writing tools that can support writing in many ways, particularly for struggling writers. They can ease the physical process of writing, enable students to produce error-free final copies, support publication, and make revision possible without tedious recopying" (p. 147). Similarly, Nagin (National Writing Project & Nagin, 2006) states, "Technology makes response, revision, and editing eminently more agreeable" (p. 29).

The difficulty of producing handwritten text was not due to a lack of ideas, but the physical strain of having to write by hand. With support, participants were able to clearly articulate ideas and watch them appear in print as they intended. My experiences with the YWs reflected Graham's (2010) assertions regarding the connection between written production and handwriting. With younger children, Graham states:

> If children cannot form letters with reasonable legibility and speed—they cannot translate the language of their minds into written text. Struggling with handwriting can lead to a self-fulfilling prophecy in which students avoid writing, come to think of themselves as not being able to write, and fall further and further behind their peers. (p. 48)

Indeed, the six boys and Jessica struggled tremendously with their handwriting. To my knowledge, the school did not have a handwriting program, but after spending countless hours in classrooms with student teachers and in observing students' writing from kindergarten to 6th grade, it was obvious that the YWs struggled more than their peers with producing legible handwriting.

With respect to using the laptop in supporting students' written production and serving as a mediating tool, I draw on Vygotsky (1934/1978) to analyze and discuss the YWs' success. Vygotsky explains that a mediating tool can be used to support an individual's learning and thinking. In this case, the laptop served as a tool to accurately and rapidly capture their ideas, thereby increasing their understanding of the writing process and elements of a narrative. With the support of the laptop, the students succeeded in producing more and higher quality writing. Their success can also be attributed to Vygotsky's theory of the "zone of proximal development," which is "the distance between the actual developmental level, as determined by independent problem solving and the level of potential development as determined through problem solving under adult guidance or in collaboration with more capable peers" (p. 86). All YWs struggled with handwriting. In fact, some commented that they could not write fast enough to get their ideas on paper, which led to frustration and ultimately quitting. They constantly asked how to spell words, which disrupted their flow of ideas. The ideas reflected in their typed narratives were indicative of their mental development—a third grader's creative ideas—and vocabulary. By supporting the YWs with tasks they could not do independently, namely typing their words, they were able to focus on higher level thinking skills, producing a narrative that reflected the qualities described in the third- and fourth-grade writing standards.

Changes in Writing: From January to July

During the after-school program all the students had their own notebooks and wrote in response to literature—their own narratives, a chapter after the final chapter in Roald Dahl's *George's Marvelous Medicine* (Dahl, 1998), and various writing prompts. I was deeply concerned about their handwriting, limited vocabulary, spelling, and punctuation. For example, Gabino was asked to think about his favorite movie, book, or video game and describe it to someone who had never seen it before. In Figure 4.1 his handwriting sample from January, before the summer after-school YWG program, contains limited details, word choice, and misspelling of words such as "allso" for "also."

Figure 4.2 shows the beginning of Gabino's narrative from the summer that he was a member of the YWG. As he dictates his words to me using my laptop, his writing sample shows more details and sophisticated terms such as "identification machine" to express his ideas.

Jessica, who often wrote a few words, rolled her notebook pages, tore them out, and threw them away, struggled the most with her writing. Her January writing sample appears in Figure 4.3. She was asked to write a summary of a short story I read aloud from a book the students chose, *Short and Shivery: Thirty Chilling Tales* (San Souci & Coville, 2001). Like Gabino, Jessica had difficulty with spelling and limited word choice before participation in the YWG.

In Figure 4.4, from the summer writing program, we see Jessica clarifying her ideas and using fairly advanced concepts such as a parent "antiquing Chinese pictures."

What is worth noting is that all words and ideas came from the YWs; I simply provided the typing to capture their words in print. Struggling writers like Gabino and Jessica seemed more willing to express their ideas through dialogue and dictation when seeing their work immediately displayed on my laptop. Hence, technology served as both a motivator and tool to limit anxiety and frustration.

FIGURE 4.1. Gabino's January Sample

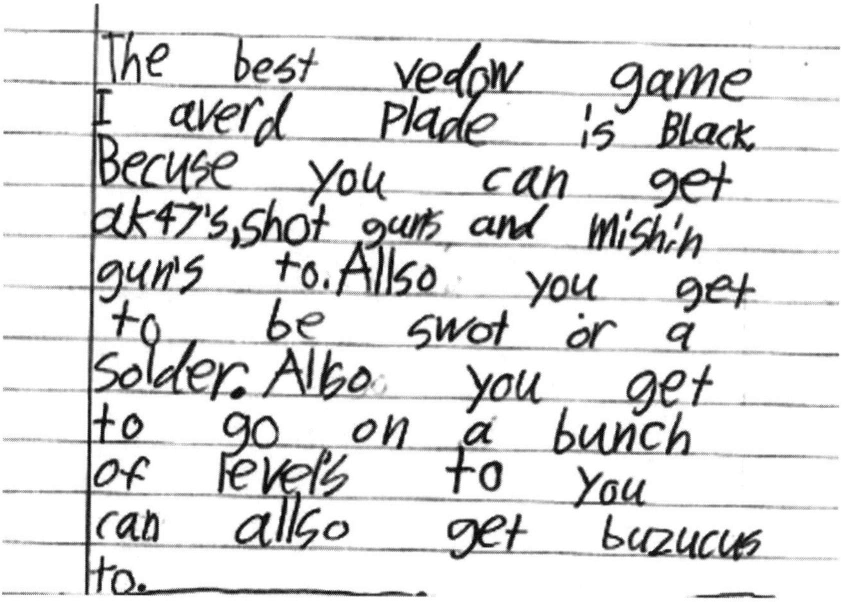

The best vedow game
I averd Plade is Black.
Becuse you can get
ak47's,shot guns and mishin
guns to. Allso you get
to be swot or a
solder. Albo you get
to go on a bunch
of levels to you
can allso get buzucus
to.

FIGURE 4.2. "Robocop Saves the Day": Gabino's Summer Sample

At work today I just made an experiment called a Cyclops," said Mr. Hankey. "Well, how did you make it?" asked Mrs. Patty "I used bubble water and fuel. First we put it in the little bottle and shook it, then we used a machine and mixed it. Then I found a little bit of sand. We put the sand in a machine then lights turned on, on the sand. Then I wore goggles and it went 'pshheeee' then we saw an animal and we named it the Cyclops," told Mr. Hankey.

Mrs. Patty, who was 50 years old, lived with Mr. Hankey in New York. She likes to write a lot and she got a job offering homes to people. She worked at an office that kids could not go in and you need a card to slide through an identification machine that opens the door. Her husband was a scientist named Mr. Hankey. He stayed in college for 2 more years when it was over, and that's how he became a good scientist. He likes to make experiments.

On Monday, June 7, 2004, they were making eggs and waffles for breakfast. Then a robber broke in their house. He was passing by their apartment and saw a servant with lobster go in. Because there were lots of things that cost money on their cart, he just broke into their house. He got the code from Mr. Hankey that was 15060. Then he found duct tape in a drawer and taped their mouths. Then he put them in a closet. He stole the safe that holds all of their jewelry and money.

FIGURE 4.3. Jessica's First Writing Sample

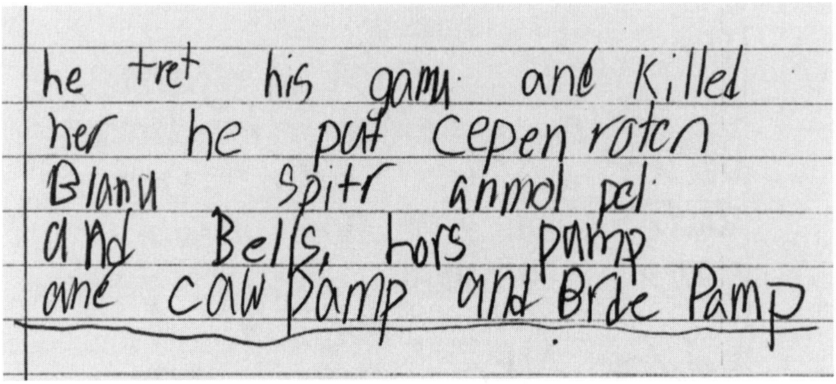
he tret his gamy and Killed
her he put cepen roten
Blanu Spitr anmol pel
and Bells, hors pamp
ane caw pamp and Brde Pamp

FIGURE 4.4. "The Kung Fu Guys": Jessica's Summer Sample

"Wow!!! She is perfect at kung fu, probably," whispered Number One.

The Kung Fu guys, who wear black belts and are from New York, found a scroll of a picture of Jessica Smith. It had her name on it and a picture of a knife with a black belt on it.

The Chinese Kung Fu guys were training the girl named Jessica. She did very well inside the training class doing kung fu fighting with her hands, legs and with big, little and all kinds of swords. They taught her how to do back flips, cartwheels, side flips and front flips. They liked training her and were trying to force her to stop hitting, but she didn't because she was too good.

They said, "Stop, stop!"

Then she said, "Okay, I will." Her mom was antiquing Chinese pictures, swords and statues and had a photograph of the Kung Fu guys. She wasn't picking up the glowing ball from Taiwan, which was at her work; because she knew it was evil. She was getting hungry, so she ordered a pizza.

Jessica was training to fight an evil glowing ball that was made out of fire. She had a necklace with a dragon and baby dragons on it that would protect her. She put on a red, yellow, black and orange glowing necklace protector that looked like a tube of toothpaste. Kung Fu fighter Number One say, "Sometimes my brother, Number Two, thinks it's toothpaste." Jessica would become evil if the stinky green gas from the fireball would go in her eyes. It was too light, if she didn't have that necklace. She didn't want to wear it because it looked ugly, but her Grandma put it on her.

CONCLUSION

On average, the number of words of the YWs' summer narratives was 477. In comparison, I selected narratives they had written independently or with a partner from January to June, which averaged 50 to 75 words. Presumably, their ideas and vocabulary had not improved so significantly in 6 months, but the emphasis on dialogue and use of the laptop as a mediating tool throughout the writing process supported the YWs in creating narratives that were a more accurate representation of their understanding of narrative, level of vocabulary, and creativity.

In a similar study on the impact of technology on the quantity of writing, Daniels (2004) found that fifth-grade students, across ability levels, produced more writing when using technology than when writing by hand. He emphasizes the importance of motivation and encourages educators to consider how to focus on the writing process with the support of technology. Specifically, he states:

> It is vital to remember that it is the writing process that concerns us the most and not the technology. Where technology is helpful we must embrace it, anywhere that it impedes or hinders writing we must oppose its use. The overwhelming amount of evidence suggests that the negative effects of computer-aided composition are minimal, and ultimately worth the risks. (p. 174)

In the YWG, participants learned that writing is a recursive rather than linear process. Each time we met, they were free to change their words and ideas rather than progress through the writing process from prewriting, to drafting, revising, editing, and finally, publishing. Each time I met with Geraldo and his partner, he would read through his draft and comment, "That doesn't make sense," and change his text until it made sense to him and his partner. Throughout the writing process, the YWs were provided support to master selected third- and fourth-grade standards because they were not hindered by their inability to use handwriting, a lower level standard, as quickly as their thoughts came to them. While we would expect students to meet and master standards as they progress, almost in a linear fashion, this is not always what occurs. Therefore, we need to identify standards they have not yet met, such as handwriting, while teaching the standards they need to learn to be prepared to progress. This requires adaptation of instruction, the use of a range of tools, and refusing to let low-level standards interfere with mastery of grade-level standards that students are capable of achieving.

Based on 16 months of data, particularly the summer session, it is clear that dialogue and technology played a critical role in achieving three outcomes: (1) Students began to view themselves as writers with important and valuable ideas; (2) the amount of text produced at the end of the YWG was a more accurate representation of their ideas; and (3) participants could focus on third- and fourth-grade standards at higher levels. The YWs' final narratives reflected the positive qualities of a hybrid. Students had opportunities to work collaboratively and independently, to construct text by hand and on the laptop, and to dictate their own ideas and those that had been tested and modified with peer support. Their final products were not simply the combination of two elements, but the best qualities from each of the elements.

The findings from this study contribute to our knowledge of effective literacy pedagogy for diverse student populations through the use of authentic reading and writing practices, technology, and dialogue/ speech. Perhaps the most important finding from the YWG was the type of learning environment we can create for students struggling to improve their understanding of literacy. In most classrooms I have visited, across districts and states with a range of student populations, and as documented in recent research, educators are frustrated with policies and mandates that allow little differentiation for those who are being left behind. By making changes that do not require extra costs, such as creating a safe and generative space for dialogue, or taking advantage of existing resources, such as basic word processing, we may be more successful in meeting the needs of our students.

During our last meeting of the summer, the YWs read their narratives aloud to the YWG, similar to the Author's Chair, an event often found in Writing Workshop (Graves & Hansen, 1983). They each received a bound publication of all the participants' narratives to share with their caregivers and teachers. When I told them we could continue the YWG in the fall, they cheered. I told them they would need to ask their caregivers for permission to continue. Nick, whose mother had made arrangements for his grandparents to pick him up each week so he could participate, said he would definitely be back. Gabino said he didn't have to ask his parents for permission because it was up to him and he would be back. Jessica followed Gabino's statement with, "Me too!" Sure enough, when we resumed the YWG in the fall, all seven students were back and excited to continue improving their literacy abilities, attitudes, and self-perceptions as capable readers and writers with important words to share with the world.

REFERENCES

Allington, R. (2002). You can't learn much from books you can't read. *Educational Leadership, 60*(3), 16–19.

Apthorp, H. S., Bodrova, E., Dean, C. B., & Florian, J. E. (2001). *Noteworthy perspectives: Teaching to the core—reading, writing, and mathematics.* Aurora, CO: Mid-Continent Research for Education and Learning.

Aukerman, M. S., Belfatti, M. A., & Santori, D. M. (2008). Teaching and learning dialogically organized reading instruction. *English Education, 40*(4), 340–364.

Barone, D., & Wright, T. E. (2008). Literacy instruction with digital and media technologies. *The Reading Teacher, 62*(4), 292–302.

Bazerman, C. (2004). Intertextualities: Volosinov, Bakhtin, literary theory, and literacy studies. In A. Ball & S. W. Freedman (Eds.), *Bakhtinian perspectives on languages, literacy, and learning* (pp. 53–65). New York, NY: Cambridge University Press.

Brown, C. A., & Dotson, K. (2007). Writing your own history: A case study using digital primary source documents. *TechTrends: Linking Research and Practice to Improve Learning, 51*(3), 30–37.

Cho, K., & Schunn, C. D. (2007). Scaffolded writing and rewriting in the disciplines: A web-based reciprocal peer review system. *Computers and Education, 48,* 409–426.

Dahl, R. (1998). *George's marvelous medicine.* New York, NY: Puffin Books.

Daniels, A. (2004). Composition instruction: Using technology to motivate students to write. *Information Technology in Childhood Education Annual,* 2004, 157–177.

Doyle, C. (1993). *The adventures of Sherlock Holmes* (Great Illustrated Classics). Edina, MN: Abdo.

Dumas, A. (2002) *The three musketeers* (Great Illustrated Classics). Edina, MN: Abdo.

Dunlap, J. C. (2006). Using guided reflective journaling activities to capture students' changing perceptions. *TechTrends: Linking Research and Practice to Improve Learning, 50*(6), 20–26.

Education Trust. (2003). *Improving your schools: A parent and community guide to No Child Left Behind.* Washington, DC: Author.

Graham, S. (2010). Want to improve children's writing? Don't neglect their handwriting. *Education Digest: Essential Readings Condensed for Quick Review, 76*(1), 49–55.

Graham, S., Harris, K. R., & Mason, L. (2005). Improving the writing performance, knowledge, and self-efficacy of struggling young writers: The effects of self-regulated strategy development. *Contemporary Educational Psychology, 30,* 207–241.

Graves, D., & Hansen, J. (1983). The author's chair. *Language Arts, 60*(2), 176–183.

Lankshear, C., & Knobel, M. (2003). *New literacies: Changing knowledge and classroom learning*. Philadelphia, PA: Open University Press.

Lantolf, J. (2000). Introducing sociocultural theory. In J. Lantolf (Ed.), *Sociocultural theory and second language learning*. Oxford, UK: Oxford University Press.

MacArthur, C. A. (2007). Best practices in teaching evaluation and revision. In S. Graham, C. MacArthur, & J. Fitzgerald (Eds.), *Best practices in writing instruction* (pp. 141–162). New York, NY: Guilford Press.

National Center for Educational Statistics (NCES). (2007a). *The nation's report card: Reading 2007*. Retrieved from http://nationsreportcard.gov/reading_2007/

National Center for Educational Statistics (NCES). (2007b). *The nation's report card: Writing*. Retrieved from. http://nationsreportcard.gov/writing_2007/

National Institute of Child Health and Human Development (NICHD). (2000). Report of the National Reading Panel. Teaching children to read: An evidence-based assessment of the scientific research literature on reading and its implications for reading instruction. Washington, DC: U.S. Government Printing Office. Retrieved from http://www.nichd.nih.gov/publications/nrp/smallbook.cfm

National Writing Project & Nagin, C. (2006). *Because writing matters: Improving student writing in our schools*. San Francisco, CA: Jossey-Bass.

Pritchard, R. J., & Honeycutt, R. L. (2007). Best practices in implementing a process approach to teaching writing. In S. Graham, C. MacArthur, & J. Fitzgerald (Eds.), *Best practices in writing instruction* (pp. 28–49). New York, NY: Guilford Press.

San Souci, R., & Coville, K. (2001). *Short & shivery: Thirty chilling tales*. New York, NY: Dell.

Stoker, B. (2005). *Dracula* (Great Illustrated Classics). Edina, MN: Abdo.

U.S. Department of Education. (2002). *No Child Left Behind*. Retrieved from http://www.ed.gov/nclb/landing.jhtml

U.S. Department of Education. (2011). *Summer 2011 EDFacts state profiles*. Washington, DC: Author. Retrieved from http://www2.ed.gov/about/inits/ed/edfacts/state-profiles/index.html

Vygotsky, L. S. (1978). *Mind in society: The development of higher psychological processes* (M. Cole, V. John-Steiner, S. Scribner, & E. Souberman, Eds. & Trans.). Cambridge, MA: Harvard University Press. (Original work published 1934)

Wells, H. G. (2002). *The invisible man* (Great Illustrated Classics). Edina, MN: Abdo.

Wenger, E. (1998). *Communities of practice: Learning, meaning, and identity*. Cambridge, UK: Cambridge University Press.

CHAPTER 5

Learning from Roberto

Scaffolding Second Language
Writing Development

Alice Quiocho
Sharon H. Ulanoff

During the 2007–08 academic year, approximately 50 million students were enrolled in U.S. schools, a number that is projected to increase to more than 53 million by 2020 (NCES, 2010). Students from ethnically and linguistically diverse backgrounds, whose numbers have increased from 9% of the student population in 1979 to 21% in 2008, consistently underperform their native-English-speaking peers (NCES, 2010). In 2009 approximately 94% of English language learners (ELLs) in the United States scored below proficient in reading in the fourth grade and 97% in 8th grade, while only 65% of their English-speaking peers in the fourth grade and 66% in the eighth grade scored below proficient in reading on the National Assessment of Educational Progress, or NAEP (NCES, 2009). These data are similar to California statistics where ELLs account for almost 25% of California's K–12 school population (Batalova & McHugh, 2010). Many ELLs simply "fall through the cracks" as a result of increased demands to learn language along with content in order to fully engage in complex learning tasks.

As educational contexts become increasingly diverse, teachers are challenged to develop expanded instructional repertoires to better meet the needs of the students they teach. These repertoires include a variety of skills and strategies that teachers use to help all students, including ELLs, gain access to the curriculum. The use of language and content *scaffolding*, a term used to connote instructional support for all students (Wood, Bruner, & Ross, 1976), can be seen as the basis for many successful practices and programs for instructing ELLs, such as the Sheltered Instruction Observation Protocol (SIOP) method (Echevarria & Graves, 2007) and the Cognitive Academic Language Learning Approach (Chamot, 2009). Such scaffolding is often used to bridge the gap between what students know and their potential to learn language (Velasco, 2010) by providing such supports as pre-teaching vocabulary, using visuals or realia, or otherwise making language comprehensible to students. However, in some classrooms, scaffolding students' learning means lowering expectations for ELLs rather than focusing on ways to make complex instructional content accessible to the students.

One of the areas where ELLs often need intensive scaffolding is writing, especially when they are learning to read and write in their second language, English. While many ELLs listen to and speak English with some ease, they are often more skilled at using communicative language and need support when it comes to academic language (August, 2008; Cummins, 2005). Because ELLs are learning to read and write concurrently with developing English proficiency, they may face many challenges beyond organization, word choice, fluency, and grammar and can benefit from language, as well as content, scaffolding to promote deep understanding of written language (Chamot, 2009; Fagan, 2003; Quiocho & Ulanoff, 2009). In addition ELLs may need one-on-one, small-group, and other intensive scaffolding to ensure that they master the decontextualized task of writing.

THE STUDY

This case study takes a close look at a fourth-grade ELL, Roberto (a pseudonym), learning in English and the ongoing dance between teacher and student as they become learners and teachers and find ways to create bridges and connect prior learning with new knowledge. We examine successful writing scaffolds that take Roberto to a different level, thus helping him "problem-solve with increasing independence on [writing] tasks that grow in difficulty" (Rodgers, 2000, p. 89). The study is guided by the following question: How does scaffolded writing instruction impact Roberto's second language writing ability? We situate our work in Roberto's classroom within the larger context of one school's reform efforts targeted at improving literacy instruction for ELLs.

We visited Roberto's classroom and Edge Lake School (ELS, a pseudonym) weekly from September 2005 to March 2006, spending

14 full school days observing Roberto's classroom, attending grade-level and schoolwide meetings, and gathering student writing samples and other classroom and school artifacts. Our days at the school usually began at 8:30 a.m. and ended at 1:00 p.m. Classroom observations were focused on examining the ways Roberto's teacher scaffolded his instruction to allow him to access the curriculum and understand complex content. We specifically looked at different strategies that his teacher used to scaffold writing instruction.

We also conducted interviews with the principal, the literacy coordinator, the Room 15 teacher, and the other fourth-grade teachers during English Language Arts (ELA) and English Language Development (ELD) instruction. Field notes were gathered during all observations and interviews; we also gathered field notes during teachers' weekly curriculum planning and debriefing meetings.

As practitioner researchers, we wanted to explore literacy-related reform efforts at the school, specifically the learning opportunities that were presented to Roberto and his classmates. We observed Roberto's class and listened to his teachers' conversations as they planned curriculum based on the California ELA and ELD standards and calibrated student writing across grade levels for ELLs. We explored issues related to access to grade-level content, consistency in grade-level curriculum, and schoolwide planning with clear cognitive and language objectives that engaged ELLs in learning grade-level content. We use Roberto's story to show his English writing development as an example of the change process at Edge Lake School.

WELCOME TO ROBERTO'S CLASS

The morning rays of the warm desert sunshine filter through the windows of Roberto's classroom, the fourth-grade classroom at Edge Lake School that we will describe in this case study. Edge Lake School, a diverse school with a population that includes 74% ELLs, was selected because it was identified as low achieving with a high administrator turnover, each of whom stayed at the school for 2 years or less. In 2004 a new principal was assigned to the school and he applied for and received a school improvement grant. The grant expired in 2005, and school staff made a commitment to continue the reform efforts using site resources and local talents. We enter Roberto's classroom one bright fall morning in 2005. The day starts with writing. His teacher, Tessie, is circulating around the room helping individual students.

Tessie: So what do you really want to say?

Roberto: I want to say like I am a Hupa boy and I want everybody to know.

Tessie: Okay, how could you say that so everyone could really know who you are and what you do?

Roberto: First I could talk about myself and my family.

Tessie: Okay, then what would you do next?

Roberto: I divide it up.

Tessie: How?

Roberto: Myself, then what I do, then what we eat, then where we live.

Tessie: Good. What next? What words could you use to help you organize?

Roberto: The transition words?

This morning Roberto just can't seem to get started as he writes a narrative pretending that he is a Hupa Indian boy. His class has been studying the history of the Hupa Indians of northern California as part of a unit on Native American history. They have been learning about the tribe's customs and lifestyles before 1850, when the gold rush brought miners to the Hoopa Valley where that tribe lived. As Roberto and Tessie talk about getting him going, soft murmurs, looks that signal "I need help," muffled giggles, and "ahas!" fill the air of Room 15.

Rubrics adorn the walls of the portable classroom. Teachers use these rubrics to analyze student work and to demonstrate expectations to the class. Students use these rubrics to guide their work and to help them show what they know in multiple ways. Two of Roberto's classmates sit at the resource center. Their eyes dart from their works in progress to the graphic organizer posted on the wall, to a dictionary in two languages and a thesaurus—heads together whispering, reading, listening, reading, and listening.

Roberto's teacher gets him started. She lets him know she is pleased because he understands that his writing will be better organized when he uses transition words. She asks Roberto to tell her some of the transition words he plans to use and he points them out to her from the word wall. He says he is ready, and Tessie moves away from Roberto's table, observes, listens, asks probing questions, makes notes, and conducts individual or small-group conferences with his classmates.

The students in Room 15 have been taught to question, reflect, read to one another, write, gaze, meander about when they need to, sit, write more, listen. It's like watching and listening to a concerto. Everyone is tuned up and ready to play—a beautiful sight to see.

THE CONTEXT FOR LEARNING IN ROOM 15

Roberto spends his days learning in Room 15 at ELS, a K–5 school in southern California, not far from the Mexican border. The school is small, with approximately 620 students. Seventy-four percent of the students in Room 15 are English ELLs like Roberto. Robert's native language is Spanish, but like the majority of ELLs in California the bulk of his instruction takes place in English as a result of legislative restrictions in place (Rumberger & Gándara, 2000). However, the teachers at ELS provide primary language (L1) support for students who are at the beginning levels of learning English as they negotiate district mandates within the school and classroom context (Pease-Alvarez, Samway, & Cifka-Herrera, 2010).

The teachers at Roberto's school made the decision to think differently about their own teaching. They knew their students could better demonstrate their knowledge about the world, the content of school, and themselves than what was seen in their standardized test scores. They believed in their students and their families. The reform efforts at ELS were led by the teachers, but fully supported by the principal. The reform process included a set of guiding principles that helped them provide equal access to the curriculum for all students (Quiocho & Ulanoff, 2009). These principles included:

- A focus on reading and writing across the curriculum. through the use of a few robust comprehension strategies that included a variety of critical thinking skills.
- A focus on ELD and ELA standards taught through standards-based topic modules developed from grade-level content standards.
- The use of content and language scaffolding throughout all lessons.
- Full participation of the site principal as colearner.

Miramontes, Nadeau, and Commins (2011) argue that the sociopolitical context of schools affects student learning. Teacher expectations, how students are placed, the manner in which the educators at a school perceive students' cultures, and the respect with which educators treat students and parents have a direct effect on student achievement (Erikson & Mohatt, 1982; Heath, 1983; McKown & Weinstein, 2008; Ogbu & Matute-Bianchi, 1986; Phillips, 1983; Skutnabb-Kangas, 1981; Trueba, 1987). The teachers at ELS decided that one of their priorities would be to involve students as partners in learning. They read the research on literacy and second language acquisition and decided that if they developed and taught a robust curriculum that integrated the critical components of interactive assessment to inform instruction, meeting state standards and raising test scores for the students would be a by-product of what happened in their classroom communities, not the goal. They would guide their students through the literacy process (Kucer, 1995). They decided to focus on writing as one means of improving reading comprehension and they implemented a cycle of observational checks, reflections, and decision making (Tierney, Crumpler, Bertelsen, & Bond, 2003).

They engaged in joint decision making that occurred at weekly grade-level meetings and, as a result of monthly professional development sessions, focused on research to inform their decisions about practice. Their reflections and conversations centered around student work, results of assessments, student portfolios, development of rubrics using district English language development standards, and comparison across grade levels by calibrating student writing. Like Garcia (2002), the teachers at Edge Lake School made the decision to "swim against the mainstream" and "examine the cultural assumptions" that had been made about their students and the assumptions that they themselves, without thinking, were making about their students.

The teachers at ELS knew that fourth graders, like Roberto, would have to write to a state-provided prompt, which is not an easy thing to do. The teachers decided that it would be difficult to write to a prompt without having everyday writing experiences to learn how to relate the part to the whole (Graves, 2004). Only then would their students be able to learn the skills of knowing what they were being asked to do in the prompt and how to get right to the point. Their students would need mentors (Corden, 2007; Fletcher, 1993). Each of the teachers would serve as mentors with high standards.

They developed other support mechanisms for students as they engaged in the writing process. By examining student assessment data, both standardized and curriculum-embedded, the teachers decided which students needed interactive writing, which ones would benefit from guided writing as a scaffold to individual writing, and which others might need to get a jump start to writing through LEA (Language Experience Approach). As Tsujimoto (2001) lit the fires of writing for his adolescent students through poetry, the teachers at ELS would start there as well (Flynn & McPhillips, 2000; Latta & Thompson, 2010; Razinski & Zimmerman, 2001).

LEARNING ABOUT ROBERTO

Roberto is a fourth-grade ELL who speaks Spanish at home. His parents are native Spanish speakers. He immigrated to the United States as a beginning third grader. As is current practice in California, the California English Language Development Test or CELDT (CDE, 2009) was administered when he first arrived at ELS to determine his language proficiency level. The CELDT is administered to students individually. For students in kindergarten and first grade the CELDT measures listening and speaking; listening, speaking, reading, and writing are assessed for students in Grades 2 and higher. Roberto was retested at the end of third grade, and his CELDT scores categorize him overall as an early intermediate ELL.

As an early intermediate reader, Roberto is expected to be able to match vocabulary words to pictures, recognize sound/symbol relationships, use context clues to choose the correct word to complete a sentence, answer some factual comprehension questions, and make inferences after reading a simple text. As an early intermediate writer, he should be able to complete a sentence using the appropriate word; respond to a picture prompt by writing words, phrases, or simple sentences that contain at least one English word spelled correctly; and write words or phrases related to the topic based on sequenced pictures and a sentence starter, although the response may contain numerous errors that distort meaning. Roberto's work demonstrates that he can indeed successfully complete all of the above tasks and much more in a supportive environment where his instruction is scaffolded in ways that promote his success. We will explore examples of his work later on in this chapter.

It is important to note that while the CELDT is used throughout California for initial identification of students' English proficiency levels, to monitor progress, and as one of four criteria for reclassification as fluent English proficient (Mora, 2005, p. 4), it does not measure content knowledge. This is problematic in that ELLs' success is often measured by their academic progress, which is dependent on their demonstrated knowledge of grade-level content. Since all assessments for ELLs measure their content knowledge in addition to their language proficiency (Mercado & Romero, 1993), it is generally difficult to evaluate whether ELLs make errors because they don't know the content or they don't have the language. Although annual language testing can inform teachers about students' language proficiency, the results alone do not help teachers understand how best to scaffold instruction to meet both students' linguistic and academic needs.

Roberto's teachers use the CELDT data along with teacher observations to plan effective instruction to help Roberto access the curriculum in order to learn content and become more proficient in English. They use strategies that focus on helping their students access the content areas so that they will succeed in learning content and language. Because Roberto's instruction is conducted in English, his second language (L2), it is up to his teacher to scaffold the curriculum in ways that promote content and language learning. We examine Roberto's work to explore how this scaffolding helps him to develop as a writer.

LEARNING FROM ROBERTO: SCAFFOLDING STRATEGIES

During writing instruction, Tessie used a variety of strategies to help Roberto and his classmates make meaning of the texts they were reading and writing, providing opportunities for ELLs to engage in instruction and demonstrate competence beyond what assessment results alone might indicate. These opportunities included a focus on comprehension throughout instruction and the use of writing scaffolds, including graphic organizers, guiding questions, rubrics, cognate and content word walls, all of which provided Roberto and his classmates with the support they needed to be successful writers. Content vocabulary, text structure, cognate transfer, and instruction in developing and using note organizers to support the writing process were also an integral part of Roberto's instruction. A high-frequency word wall was also visible in the classroom for student use during the editing process.

Roberto was further supported in learning grade-level content during ELD time (content previously taught in reading/language arts is reviewed, retaught, and extended). During ELD time all students write about the content studied in class. In the afternoons students are mixed in extended classes where students who speak Spanish as a primary language and English as a second language at different levels sit with native English speakers. Throughout this time there are lessons about text structure, syntactical structure, and additional comprehension strategies such as inferential thinking and metacognition where students are taught to think explicitly about the specific literacy task in which they are engaged. Students also have opportunities to do more writing while receiving feedback from peers and teachers.

Samples of Roberto's writing were collected from September 2005 to March 2006. Tessie's goal was for Roberto and the rest of her students to develop conceptual understanding through the use of scaffolded content area reading and writing. During instruction she focused on organization, completeness of thought, and the ability to communicate complete thoughts, since Roberto and the other ELLs in Room 15 are learning to express themselves in their second language. We use descriptions of writing activities and excerpts from Roberto's writing samples from September to March to demonstrate how his teacher consistently scaffolded reading and writing instruction to promote learning.

Scaffolds for Teaching and Learning Poetry

Roberto's teacher, Tessie, and the literacy coordinator, Kris, engage the students in poetry writing throughout the year because they know that students can write poetry without worrying about structure and form. Like the ELLs who Koch and Padgett (1999) worked with in New York, the students in Tessie's class can experiment with language, using their primary language mixed with English in their poems to construct meaning, without worrying about punctuation and syntax. Since poetry is often written in free form, its use allows students to take risks in writing without focusing on form. Tessie connects poetry writing to content themes linked to state standards.

To prepare her students to work as poets, Tessie uses poetry read-alouds to encourage them to listen to the "music" and "wondrous words" in language and read like a writer (Ray, 1999; Smith, 1988). In addition to books related to the current content theme, there is a large collection of poetry books in the classroom, which many students read during independent reading time.

Roberto and his classmates are further encouraged to investigate poetry by creating personal poetry books, filled with self-authored poems. By October, Roberto's personal poetry book contained 10 poems. Some of the poems are pattern poems while others are based on published poems, which serve as mentor texts for his writing (Corden, 2007). For example, following an example in Cullinan, Scala, and Schroder (1995), when Tessie used "The Galapagos Tortoise" by Georgia Heard (1992) as the basis for collaborative poetry writing during a unit on endangered species, Roberto and a classmate penned the following poem:

Will we ever see a butterfly again
With its silver spots?

Will we ever see the northern spotted owl
Is he gone forever?
Or a Fresno Kangaroo rat
Looking for his food?

Or a Guadalupe fur seal
Is he now a lady's coat?

Or see a desert tortoise
Who was taken from his home in Sonora?

This science unit raised students' curiosity about animals and why they disappear or become endangered. During lessons students learned that animals can become scarce or have their appearances change when people overhunt or move them from one environment to another, because the relocation of animals such as the desert tortoise was perceived as a threat to other animals' habitats such as rats, goats, or pigs. Tessie told Roberto and his classmates that sometimes people moved tortoises to the city because there were too many of them in the Sonora desert. "So, do they ever come back?" the students asked. "Sometimes," their teacher replied, "but not always." The poem above demonstrates the connections students made between what they had learned and the preferred writing mode Tessie often selected for her ELL students: poetry.

Integrated Instruction

Linking Science and Writing. We observed Roberto and his class during a lesson on poetry writing within the context of an integrated, thematic, standards-based unit where Tessie was using science concepts to teach during the language arts period. The students had been studying vertebrates and invertebrates and were intrigued about the difference between lizards and snakes. To begin this lesson, Tessie selects a nonfiction book about snakes and engages students in an interactive read-aloud, comparing snakes with lizards as the class discusses the book. She reads small chunks of informational text, stopping to ask pairs of students to retell what she reads. Next, Tessie shows the class pictures of lizards with legs and lizards without legs. Then she

FIGURE 5.1. Roberto's Snake Poem from September

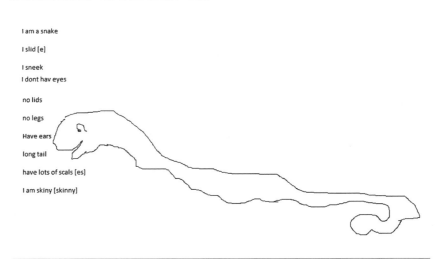

I am a snake
I slid [e]
I sneek
I dont hav eyes
no lids
no legs
Have ears
long tail
have lots of scals [es]
I am skiny [skinny]

tells the class that snakes are *like* legless lizards but that there were some differences.

After discussing in pairs, the students share with the class while the teacher writes their novel ideas on an informational chart about snakes. Tessie then sends the students back to their desks to compose their own poems. As students begin to write, they refer back to this chart and the cognate (English-Spanish words) or content word walls that are present in the classroom while Tessie circulates around the room. At the end of the lesson, students are asked to draw one of the following: a legless lizard, a lizard with legs, or a snake and then write another poem about the characteristics of the chosen animal.

While other students write poems about what they learned about snakes and lizards, Roberto draws a snake, which is very, very light, and almost a scribble, and initially adds his poem to a dialogue box that comes out of the snake's mouth, as if he were the snake speaking. His poem contains some misperceptions about snakes, such as "I don't have eyes," and limited facts about snakes. When Roberto completed his hand-drawn work, we created an electronic version with the poem typed beside the snake (see Figure 5.1).

Tessie and her colleagues had spoken many times of the various ways poetry could be used to support the academic language learning of ELLs. They observed that the rhythm of poetry was something to which ELL students were attracted. They loved reading poetry, collecting favorite poems, and writing poetry as well. Tessie and her colleagues also learned by watching their students that at the very beginning of learning English as a second language, students could draw and write descriptive words that served as a scaffold for future poetry. This phase of language development based on teacher observation is what the snake picture poem represents. (In terms of time of the year, the snake picture poem was drawn first and the poetry about the endangered species occurred later in the school year.)

Linking Social Studies and Writing. During another lesson Tessie uses social studies as a focus for content area writing instruction, teaching a variety of strategies, including the use of graphic organizers, such as Venn diagrams, as ways to understand expository structures. Tessie knows that using graphic organizers will help students sort out their thinking about the topic being studied. She models these strategies and works with the class to create graphic organizers to serve as models for the students' individual work. She starts with oral language development related to accessing prior knowledge from the books they have already read. There is a large cognate word wall on one side of the room and Tessie makes connections and adds words from Spanish-English such as "accidente—accident," "historia—history," and "animal—animal" that will help her students with the writing task. Students also add words and then use the word wall to create their own graphic organizers to guide their writing. The word wall helps them to remember key ideas they will use in their writing. Tessie tells us, "We use the graphic organizers for three main reasons: to review oral language, to record important ideas, and to help preserve the academic language that students can use in their writing."

As students begin working, Roberto creates a Venn diagram comparing and contrasting rain forests and deserts, although he only lists the differences between the two. His list of characteristics about the desert includes words and phrases he either remembers or copies from the class graphic organizer: "dry all year"; "lots of animals live there"; "(small) animals live"; "cat die"; "bushies under ground"; "eat leaves and fruit seeds"; "other animals"; "little water to drink"; and "get wonder." The rain forest list contains one complete communicative thought in "wet and warm all year." Other phrases have no subject or noun, so it is unclear what or who Roberto refers to when he writes: "live in trees," "hunt on ground," "lots of water to drink."

Roberto uses his graphic organizer to construct complete sentences, writing two that contain information not found in the graphic organizer. The first sentence is "Desert as [has] no water because it does not rain there and they have durt [dirt] shack." Roberto clearly uses other resources to scaffold his writing, including small-group and whole-class discussions. His listening skills serve him well as he works at learning grade-level content. His next sentence about the rain forest demonstrates content knowledge: "Rain forest ass [has] lots of animals because there [they] are odopd [adapted] were [where] they live." According to Tessie, "[Roberto] tries really hard. He struggles with learning this second language. Writing is hard, but he'll get better the more he writes. But, the ideas are there and they are accurate."

Tessie understands that comparison/contrast is a difficult structure for her students, particularly for ELLs like Roberto. She searches for ways to scaffold the curriculum to provide access to grade-level content, based on the background knowledge that each student brings to the learning, stating:

> Our kids really know so much. Like on our recent trip to Olvera St. in Los Angeles. The guide was explaining to the students about how Los Angeles began. He also talked about the role of the missionaries in the settlement. My kids chimed in with accurate facts and he told me that he had never had a class that knew so much. So it matters that we have our students learn content and write about it. It supports their academic language development.

Roberto later produces a learning log entry as a follow-up to this trip, attempting to write about animals in early Los Angeles, but confusing them with other animals, "I lurned that sum animals are very dangerous like radle snacks and I lurned how baby animals came out from big giraffe and I lurned that giraffe eat leafe from trees." In this log Roberto uses developmental spelling, such as "lurned" for *learned* where the *ea* is not an easily transferable vowel diagraph from another language that has no diagraphs. He also uses the word *and* to join three ideas, which is developmental for ELLs and native English speakers. Roberto listens to read-alouds, class discussions, and information shared by the teacher, and uses this material in his writing. Instead of focusing on mechanics, he concentrates on communicating content in his writing.

During a unit on Native American history, part of the fourth-grade social studies curriculum, Roberto writes from the perspective of a Mojave boy from the 1800s. The students have been studying the Native Americans of the Mojave Desert, the Serrano tribe from the San Bernardino Mountains, within the context of California history. Roberto's sample is the result of several drafts and conferences with peers and the teacher, and was completed during several lessons. He begins by explaining the identity of the "author" of the piece. "My name is running horse. They call me running horse because I like to run and I like horses. My tribe is the Mohaves. I am ten years old . . . " Although some of the sentences are repetitious, which is common with emerging writers, Roberto goes on to give more description, elaborating on his chores, where he lives, and how his family hunts for food, presenting a picture for the reader. "We live in [a] rectangular house. [Our] roof is made of mud. Are roof is made of mud because it ceps [keeps] the hot sun away. The side of [our] house are left open. They are left open so the breeze comes in." Roberto demonstrates his growth as a writer and the connections he makes between literature and history. In this piece he shows that he is able to adopt the perspective of a character linked to social studies content, a valuable skill that supports the process of developing inferential thinking as well as responding to literature (Vacca & Vacca, 2001). Although his piece is a fictional narrative, Roberto provides the reader with details from his studies about the Mojave tribes, indicating that he understands that a writer needs to support statements with details that can be substantiated. Compared to his first poem of the year (Figure 5.1), this sample contains 236 words and 23 complete ideas; the growth is evident.

Using Guiding Questions, Prompts, and Rubrics

Tessie provides Roberto with guiding questions that encourage reflection during writing tasks such as journal writing or literature response. The guiding questions facilitate his success in adding this type of writing to his repertoire. She also provides reflective questions about the writing process for students to use as they write and models how to use the questions, for example, "Is my paper easy to read? Did I become the person in history? Did I say what I wanted to say?" The questions help students think about their writing while they write and demonstrate the kinds of questions to ask peers when they need help.

In addition to guiding questions, Tessie provides the class with rubrics that spell out the expectations for the writing task. For example, Roberto and his teacher use an analytical rubric to support the comparison/contrast structure, guide the writing process, and evaluate the finished products (see Figure 5.2). This is one of many rubrics used throughout the school year and all rubrics use language that is accessible to students as well as the teacher. Additionally, students are taught how to read and use rubrics before they begin writing. If there is confusion about any specific rubric, the teacher rewrites it based on

FIGURE 5.2. Student-Friendly Rubric About Analysis

Read the questions. Remember that your writing must answer the Who? What? Where? When? How? questions and give details. How did it look? Sound? Smell? Taste? Feel?

Here are some examples. You may use the examples and add your own words.

Question	Examples
Where does this all take place?	On a beautiful spring morning
	On a hot, dusty afternoon in the summertime
	In the cold, cold, chilling wind of winter
What are we talking about?	A man who is looking for something to do
	A little boy who wants to find his friend and not wait
	The explorers want to go find new things and places
Who was there?	The man and his friends went out looking for something to do
	A little boy whistled to his dog and they went to find his friend
	The explorers and the crew of sailors went forth on the open sea
What did they do?	The man went out with his friends to find something to do because he was bored
	A little boy whistled to his dog and they went to find his lost friend
	The explorers and the crew of sailors left the dock and sailed into the open sea
What words could be used to describe the people?	The old, sad man and his best friends
	A lonely little boy and his white fluffy dog
	The eager explorers and the noisy crew of sailors
What words could be used to describe how they are doing something?	Eagerly searched for something to do
	Searched for their friend with fear
	Bravely set sail on the open sea
Now try to put the sentences together.	One beautiful morning a sad old man and his best friends eagerly searched for something to do.

Have you tried to build your sentences using Who? Where? When? Why? How?

Have you included descriptive words to help us see the people and things?

Have you used words to help us see the action?

student feedback. All "student-friendly" rubrics are posted on large charts in the front of the classroom for student viewing and use.

WHAT DID WE LEARN FROM ROBERTO AND HIS TEACHERS?

We learned a good deal about supporting ELLs in writing from Roberto and his teachers, including how important it is to observe students in classrooms, analyze their work, and watch and learn from them and their teachers. As we describe promising instructional practices that consistently support ELLs in schools and demonstrate their improved academic achievement, we hope that others will be able to make sense of the lessons we've learned. It is only when we understand students' strengths and needs that we can work toward making connections between what they bring to school and what they need to learn. We can then use students' strengths to support them and provide them with access to grade-level content using assessment results as starting points.

REFERENCES

August, D. (2008). *Integrating English language learners into district-instructional programs.* Paper presented at the annual Bilingual, Immigrant, and Refugee Education Directors' Meeting, Austin, TX. Retrieved from www.cgcs.org/conferences/BIRE08_Presentation2.ppt

Batalova, J., & McHugh, M. (2010). States and Districts with the highest number and share of English language learners. *ELL Information Center Fact Sheet Series #2.* Washington, DC: Migration Policy Institute. Retrieved from http://www.migrationinformation.org/ellinfo/FactSheet_ELL2.pdf

California Department of Education (CDE). (2009). *California English language development test (CELDT): Understanding and using 2009–10 individual results.* Sacramento: Author. Retrieved from http://www.cde.ca.gov/ta/tg/el/documents/celdt09astpkt1.pdf

Chamot, A. U. (2009). *The CALLA handbook: Implementing the cognitive academic language learning approach* (2nd ed.). Boston, MA: Pearson.

Corden, R. (2007). Developing reading-writing connections: The impact of explicit instruction of literary devices on the quality of children's narrative writing. *Journal of Research in Childhood Education, 21*(3), 269–289.

Cullinan, B. E., Scala, M. C., & Schroder, V. C. (1995). *Three voices: An invitation to poetry across the curriculum.* York, ME: Stenhouse.

Cummins, J. (2005). Teaching the language of academic success: A framework for school-based language policies. In C. F. Leyba (Ed.), *Schooling and language minority students: A theoretico-practico framework* (pp. 3–32). Los Angeles, CA: LBD.

Echevarria, J., & Graves, A. (2007). *Sheltered content instruction: Teaching English language learners with diverse abilities* (3rd ed.). Boston, MA: Allyn & Bacon.

Erikson, F., & Mohatt, G. (1982). Cultural organization of participation structures in two classrooms of Indian students. In G. Spindler (Ed.), *Doing the ethnography of schooling: Educational anthropology in action* (pp. 132–174). New York, NY: Holt, Rinehart & Winston.

Fagan, B. (2003). Scaffolds to help ELL readers. *Voices from the Middle, 11*(1), 38–42.

Fletcher, R. (1993). *What a writer needs.* Portsmouth, NH: Heinemann.

Flynn, N., & McPhillips, S. (2000). *A note slipped under the door: Teaching from poems we love.* York, ME: Stenhouse.

Garcia, K. (2002). *Swimming against the mainstream: Examining cultural assumptions in the classrooms.* In L. Darling-Hammond, J. French, & S. P. Garcia-Lopez (Eds.), *Learning to teach for social justice* (pp. 22–29). New York, NY: Teachers College Press.

Graves, D. (2004). *Teaching day by day: 180 stories to help you along the way.* Portsmouth, NH: Heinemann.

Heard, G. (1992). The Galapagos tortoise. *Creatures of earth, sea, and sky.* Honesdale, PA: Boyds Mills Press.

Heath, S. B. (1983). *Ways with words: Language, life and work in communities and classrooms.* Cambridge, UK: Cambridge University Press.

Koch, K., & Padgett, R. (1999). *Wishes, lies and dreams: Teaching children to write poetry.* New York: Harper Perrenial.

Kucer, S. B. (1995). Guiding bilingual students "through" the literacy process. *Language Arts, 72*(1), 20–29.

Latta, M. M., & Thompson, C. M. (2010). Voices of resistance, voices of transcendence: Musicians as models of the poetic-political imagination. *International Journal of Education and the Arts, 11*(3), 1–24.

McKown, C., & Weinstein, R. S. (2008). Teacher expectations, classroom context, and the achievement gap. *Journal of School Psychology, 46,* 235–261.

Mercado, C., & Romero, M. (1993). Assessment of students in bilingual education. In M. B. Arias & U. Casanova (Eds.), *Bilingual education: Politics, practice, research* (pp. 144–170). Chicago, IL: University of Chicago Press.

Miramontes, O. B., Nadeau, A., & Commins, N. L. (2011). *Restructuring schools for linguistic diversity: Linking decision making to effective programs* (2nd ed.). New York, NY: Teachers College Press.

Mora, J. K. (2005). *The truth about the CELDT: California English Language Development Test.* Retrieved from http://www.moramodules.com/Prop227/celdt.htm

National Center for Education Statistics (NCES). (2009). *NAEP data explorer results: National assessment of educational progress 2009 reading assessment:.* Retrieved from http://nces.ed.gov/nationsreportcard/naepdata/report.aspx

National Center for Education Statistics (NCES). (2010). *The condition of education 2010.* Washington, DC: Author.

Ogbu, J., & Matute-Bianchi, M. E. (1986). Understanding sociocultural factors: Knowledge, identity and school adjustment. In California Department of Education (Eds.), *Beyond language: Social and cultural factors in schooling language minority students* (pp. 73–142). Los Angeles, CA: Evaluation, Dissemination, and Assessment Center.

Pease-Alvarez, L., Samway, K. D., & Cifka-Herrera, C. (2010). Working within the system: Teachers of English learners negotiating a literacy instruction mandate. *Language Policy, 9,* 313–334. doi 10.1007/s10993-010-9180-5

Phillips, S. U. (1983). *The invisible culture: Communication in classroom and community on the Warm Springs Indian reservation.* Prospect Heights, IL: Waveland Press.

Quiocho, A., & Ulanoff, S. H. (2009). *Differentiating literacy instruction for English language learners.* Boston, MA: Allyn & Bacon.

Ray, K. W. (1999). *Wondrous words: Writers and writing in the elementary classroom.* Urbana, IL: National Council of Teachers of English.

Razinski. T., & Zimmerman, B. S. (2001). *Phonics poetry: Teaching word families.* Boston, MA: Allyn & Bacon.

Rodgers, E. M. (2000). Language matters: When is a scaffold really a scaffold? *National Reading Conference Yearbook, 49,* 78–90.

Rumberger, R. W., & Gándara, P. (2000). Crucial issues in California Education: The schooling of English learners. *UC LMRI Newsletter, 9*(3), 1–2.

Skutnabb-Kangas, T. (1981). *Bilingualism or not: The education of minorities.* Clevedon, UK: Multilingual Matters.

Smith, F. (1988). *Insult to intelligence: The bureaucratic invasion of our classrooms* (Rev. ed.). Portsmouth, NH: Heinemann.

Tierney, R. J., Crumpler, T. P., Bertelsen, C. D., & Bond, E. L. (2003). *Interactive assessment: Teachers, parents and students as partners.* Boston: Christopher-Gordon.

Trueba, H. (1987). *Raising silent voices: Educating the linguistic minorities for the 21st century.* New York, NY: Newbury House.

Tsujimoto, J. (2001). *Lighting fires: How the passionate teacher engages adolescent writers.* Portsmouth, NH: Heinemann.

Vacca, R. T., & Vacca, J. A. L. (2001). *Content area reading: Literacy and learning across the curriculum* (7th ed.). Boston, MA: Allyn & Bacon.

Velasco, P. (2010). Indigenous students in bilingual Spanish–English classrooms in New York: A teacher's mediation strategies. *International Journal of Sociological Language, 2010*(206), 255–271.

Wood, D. J., Bruner, J. S., & Ross, G. (1976). The role of tutoring in problem solving. *Journal of Child Psychology and Psychiatry, 17*(2), 89–100.

CHAPTER 6

Cognate Strategy Instruction

Providing Powerful Literacy Tools to
Spanish-Speaking Students

Shira Lubliner
Dana L. Grisham

> *I wish I had been taught to use cognates much sooner because it would have*
> *made reading English so much easier. I didn't learn to recognize cognates until I*
> *was in college and, even then, I didn't use it as well as I might have.*

Bilingual graduate student, 2006

Marta Gonzales (all names of students and teachers are pseudonyms), the Latina student quoted above, is a successful student in the Graduate Reading Program in an urban California university. She is also a successful teacher who, like many of us, faces the daily challenge of teaching reading effectively in our increasingly diverse classrooms. Marta remembers how quickly she learned to speak English and how slowly she learned to make sense of her academic texts. She also remembers gradually realizing that she could use her knowledge of Spanish to understand academic English. This insight came to Marta late in her academic career. No one taught her to recognize and apply the similarities in words to understand what she was reading in her second language, English. Through her graduate studies in reading, Marta has come to understand the systematic nature of cognate study and plans to apply it in her classroom.

Cognates are words that are spelled similarly in Spanish and English and share meaning due to a common Latin root. Cognates are particularly plentiful in content area texts such as social studies and science books. For example, the word *nation* in English is *nación* in Spanish. Not all words that look and sound alike are cognates. The word *rope* in English has no relationship to the word *ropa* (clothes) in Spanish. Context is an important part of the strategic use of cognates.

Marta's students are fortunate to have a bilingual Spanish-speaking teacher who understands the power of the cognate strategy. Teachers like Marta can point out cognates in texts and model the processes of cross-linguistic transfer for their students. But only a small percentage of Spanish-speaking students have teachers conversant in Spanish. The vast majority of Spanish-speaking students are in mainstream classes with monolingual English-speaking teachers. California, for example, has the largest population of English language learners (ELLs) in the country, 84.5% of whom speak Spanish as their first language. Only 6.5% of California ELLS receive bilingual instruction for core academic subjects (Jepsen & Alth, 2005). Teachers are responsible for meeting the needs of ELLs in their classrooms even though many of these teachers are not bilingual, or have minimal skills in languages other than English. ELLs rely on their teachers to help them acquire the vast number of words necessary to comprehend English texts and succeed in school.

Children who enter school knowing fewer words find learning to read much more difficult than children with well-developed vocabulary (Chall, Jacobs, & Baldwin, 1990; Stanovich, 1986). The achievement gap is wider with students from economically disadvantaged backgrounds and for students whose first language (L1) is not English. Spanish-speaking students, a group whose underachievement is of serious concern to educators, are the fastest growing group of children in American schools (Tabors, Páez, & López, 2003). As noted by Quiocho and Ulanoff in Chapter 5, only a small percentage of Latino fourth-grade students score at the proficient or advanced levels in reading, compared to White students. Although Latino achievement on state and national assessments such as the National Assessment of Educational Progress (NAEP) has risen during the past decade, the achievement gap remains a major concern (NCES, 2009). It is clear that educational interventions must be designed to strengthen the reading achievement of Latino students, particularly those who are not yet fluent in English, if we are to narrow the achievement gap.

The magnitude of the vocabulary gap between ELLs and English-speaking students is staggering. Researchers estimate that the average student learns 3,000 words per year and knows approximately 10,000 words by the end of third grade and 40,000 words by the end of high school (Nagy, 1986; Nagy, Herman, & Anderson, 1985). How can we help ELLs catch up? We have to teach ELLs a vast number of English words, particularly content area vocabulary words so that they can understand the books they are required to read in school. Fortunately,

Spanish-speaking students have an advantage, as English and Spanish share more than 20,000 cognates (Montelongo, Hernandez, & Herter, 2009). An analysis of the Academic Word List (Coxhead, 2000) revealed that approximately 70% of the 570 word families used frequently in academic texts are English-Spanish cognates (Hiebert & Lubliner, 2008; Lubliner & Hiebert, 2011).

Research has shown that successful bilingual students use cognates to help them in English reading comprehension tasks (García, 1999; Jimenez, García, & Pearson, 1996; Proctor, Dalton, & Grisham, 2007; Proctor & Mo, 2009). But this ability to recognize cognates and transfer word knowledge across languages is more complex than it appears. As the quote at the beginning of this article demonstrates, cognate recognition is not automatic for students. In fact, researchers have noted that Spanish-speaking students do not recognize most of the cognates they encounter in English texts (García, 1999; Nagy, García, Durguno lu, & Hancin-Bhatt, 1993). García pointed out that students need explicit instruction in cognates if they are to utilize their knowledge of Spanish in English reading tasks.

COGNATE STRATEGY INSTRUCTION

Cognate Strategy Instruction (CSI) is a program developed by Lubliner (2005) that includes explicit instruction in cognate recognition and the strategic procedures designed to facilitate cross-linguistic transfer of vocabulary knowledge. The purpose of the CSI program was to determine whether providing Spanish-speaking bilingual students with this instruction would increase their vocabulary and ability to understand English texts. We also wanted to know whether teachers would benefit from exposure to a new way of conceptualizing and teaching academic English in relationship to Spanish cognates.

This CSI research project took place during the 2006–07 academic year. We recruited three fifth-grade teachers with a high percentage of Spanish-speaking students at a Title I elementary school in northern California. Sixty-five out of 70 participating students were classified as ELLs, nearly all of whom spoke Spanish as their L1. Two of the teachers, Ms. Adams and Ms. Baker, were monolingual, and one teacher, Ms. Carter, was a nonnative-Spanish-speaking bilingual. The teachers had similar backgrounds. All were certificated in California and were novices (less than 3 years of teaching experience). All of them were eager to learn new methods that could be used to improve the achievement of their Latino students.

We met several times with the teachers after school and provided them with a teacher's guide that was not scripted, but contained 20 cognate lessons aligned to their social studies textbooks (Porter et al., 2007). We spent time discussing the methods of instruction outlined in the teacher's guide and encouraged the teachers to collaborate on implementation. The monolingual teachers admitted to having some uneasiness about using Spanish, a language that they did not speak. The Spanish-speaking teacher quickly took the lead and offered to help her colleagues with implementing CSI instruction.

The school's reading specialist, Ms. Morris, who was also an instructor at our university, was an active participant in the CSI project. Ms. Morris monitored fidelity of implementation by observing many of the lessons and sharing her comments and concerns with us. In response to her feedback, the CSI materials were frequently revised to better meet the needs of the teachers and their students.

Several challenges became apparent as we worked with teachers on the development of materials and implementation of the CSI project. We found that Spanish literacy is an important determinant of children's ability to recognize cognates. Children without L1 language literacy had never seen the Spanish equivalent of English words in print. Consequently, they did not recognize cognates, even those that were identical in spelling to words that they knew in Spanish (e.g., *animal/ animal*). This led to the realization that instruction must help students identify words that sound alike in English and Spanish as well as words that are spelled in a similar way. We developed lessons to help students recognize phonological similarities and differences in cognate patterns.

A second challenge was related to the development of Spanish-speaking children's academic vocabulary. Many children, particularly those from less literate homes, are only exposed to academic vocabulary at school. If Latino children do not know the meaning of a word in Spanish, the fact that it is a cognate is of little help in understanding the English word encountered in a text. We were very concerned about this; however, an analysis conducted by Lubliner and Hiebert (2011) determined that many cognates are asymmetrical in terms of frequency. Academic English words are often much less frequent than their cognate equivalents in Spanish. For example, the word *edifice* is rare in English, but the cognate, *edificio* is a very common Spanish word. This asymmetrical frequency pattern may provide Spanish-speaking students with a significant advantage in acquiring academic English vocabulary.

Another challenge was the teachers' fear that false cognates would distract and confuse the students. In order to assuage their concerns, we reviewed the first chapters of the fifth-grade science and social studies textbooks. We found hundreds of cognates and only a few examples of what might be called "partial cognates"—words that share partial, but not exact, meaning in Spanish and English. We shared our results with the teachers, explaining that the challenge posed by "false cognates" is exaggerated.

The CSI lessons were based on the Catch a Cognate Cue Card (Lubliner, 2005) and instructional activities for 20 high-frequency cognate patterns. The first CSI lesson was inductive in nature, designed to introduce the concept of cognates and to build the students' interest. The following is a description of a lesson delivered by Ms. Adams, one of the monolingual English-speaking teachers that we observed.

Sample Lesson on Introducing the Concept of Cognates: Ms. Adams

Ms. Adams began by placing a list of English words on the overhead (such as group, activity, no, family, education) and asked the students, "What do these words have in common?" The students read the words and talked quietly in their table groups. Before long, most of the groups had figured out that all of the words were similar in Spanish and English (*group/grupo, no/no, activity/actividad, family/familia, education/educación*). Using the CSI teacher's guide, Ms. Adams introduced the term *cognate* and explained that it applies to Spanish and English words that look similar and share a common Latin root. She pointed to the word *manual* and asked the students to think of a word in Spanish that is similar to *manual*. The Latino students quickly noted the similarity between *manual* and *mano*, the Spanish word for "hand." Ms. Adams explained that Spanish-speakers have an advantage in learning sophisticated Latin-based vocabulary because many of these words are much more common in Spanish than in English. She told the students, "You are so lucky you know Spanish! Spanish is a lot closer to Latin than English, so it's much easier for you to learn these hard words that come from Latin (academic vocabulary) than for kids who just speak English."

Ms. Adams provided a rationale for cognate instruction, explaining that between one third and one half of the words that the students would encounter in their content area textbooks would be similar in Spanish and English (Nash, 1997). Ms. Adams encouraged the students to think of additional cognates, resulting in an enthusiastic dialogue in two languages and many additions to the cognate list. Although the lesson was somewhat uncomfortable for Ms. Adams because she was a monolingual English-speaking teacher, she reported that the Spanish-speaking students were eager to take the lead on cognate activities.

Sample Lesson on Recognizing Specific Cognate Patterns: Ms. Baker

We observed the next lesson, which was focused on teaching students to recognize specific cognate patterns, in Ms. Baker's class. The teacher (also monolingual English-speaking) used a chart of 20 patterns with a list of cognates sorted by pattern from the teacher's guide. She placed the cognate pattern chart on the overhead and explicitly taught each cognate pattern. When she came to the *ion*-pattern words, Ms. Baker said:

> Boys and girls, take a look at these two words: *nation/nación*. What differences do you see in the spelling of the words in English [pointing to *nation*] and Spanish [pointing to *nación*]? They look pretty similar, don't they? Only the letter *t* and the accent are different. Now, I want you to listen carefully as I say the English word and Jose [a student volunteer] says the Spanish word —*nay*-shun, na-see-*ohn*. Do they sound alike? [The students shake their heads.] No, they don't sound alike at all. In English we say "shun" for the *-tion* ending, but in Spanish you say "see-ohn." Just about all of the words that end in *-ion* are cognates that follow this same pattern.

Ms. Baker invited the students to think of additional cognates that followed the ion pattern. The students caught on quickly and were soon calling out a multitude of words such as *addition, education,* and *division*. As she moved through the list, Ms. Baker sometimes appeared unsure as to whether the students' examples were accurate, but the students corrected each other and produced cognate lists that the Spanish-speaking teacher later deemed acceptable. Ms. Baker used resources that she found on a website (http://www.cognates. org, which used to provide lists of cognates) in addition to words we provided in the teacher's guide. The chart of cognate patterns used for this lesson can be found in Figure 6.1. The last column shows a partial list of words that the students suggested, with coaching from the teacher.

Strategic Aspects of Cognate Strategy Instruction

The second professional development meeting focused on the strategic aspects of CSI. Lubliner began with a discussion linking CSI to the large body of cognitive strategy research that identifies the processes that skilled readers use and breaks down these skills so that they can be taught to less skilled readers (Brown, 1985; Brown & Palincsar, 1986; Dole, Brown, & Trathen, 1996; Palincsar, 1983, 1984, 1985, 1986; Palincsar & Brown, 1985; Weinstein & Mayer, 1986). We told the teachers that CSI methods are based on the strategies used by successful bilingual students as they transfer word meaning across languages. Cross-language transfer entails the use of metacognitive skills (the ability to monitor thinking) and metalinguistic skills (the ability to monitor and manipulate language). We explained that our goal was to enable all of the bilingual students to master the cognate strategy. This process would entail teaching students the following series of tasks: monitoring comprehension of English texts during reading; stopping when an unknown word is encountered; recognizing that the word has a Spanish equivalent; retrieving the meaning of the Spanish word from memory; and applying the Spanish word meaning to the task of text comprehension.

Teaching cognitive strategies is challenging for teachers. This is particularly so in the case of monolingual teachers who must provide instruction based, in part, on an unfamiliar language. To support the monolingual teachers, the third professional development session focused on the integration of CSI guidelines and the Catch a Cognate Cue Card (Lubliner, 2005). During the meeting we discussed with the teachers the importance of building metacognitive and metalinguistic skills by encouraging students to think about words. Then we encouraged the teachers to find cognates we had listed in the social studies chapter and to practice providing cognate instruction to each other. The goal of the professional development process was to ensure that teachers were able to use CSI independently after the project had concluded. We wanted them to "own" CSI.

The Catch a Cognate Cue Card. Because complex cognitive strategies can be difficult, a number of researchers have suggested using cue cards to scaffold student learning (Bereiter & Bird, 1985). Lubliner provided a Catch a Cognate Cue Card (Lubliner, 2005) to be used as a basis of CSI lessons (see Figure 6.2).

CSI Guidelines. We reviewed the Catch a Cognate Cue Card with the teachers and provided them with a set of guidelines (see Figure 6.3) designed to strengthen their ability to teach the cognate strategy. We explained that cognitive strategies require explicit instruction and a great deal of modeling and coaching.

FIGURE 6.1. Common English/Spanish Cognate Patterns

Pattern	Orthographic Shifts from English to Spanish	Pattern Examples	Add Your Own Examples
1. Same: misc.	Words are spelled the same in English and Spanish (accents don't count as differences).	area/área	no/no, Mexico/México, America/América,
2. Same: -al, -il	Words ending with -al, -il are spelled the same in English and Spanish.	animal/animal	total/total, hospital/hospital
3. Same: -ar, -or	Words ending with -ar, -or are spelled the same in English and Spanish.	popular/popular, color/color	motor/motor, actor/actor
4. Same: -able, -ible	Words ending with -able, -ible are spelled the same in English and Spanish.	visible/visible	terrible/terrible, possible/posible
5. Add and change	-a, -o, -e may be added to the end of the Spanish word; internal letters may be dropped or changed.	fruit/fruta, group/grupo, art/arte	grade/grado, American/Americano, class/clase
6. -ory, -ary, -ery	Words ending with -ory, -ary, -ery in English change to -ario, -aria ending in Spanish.	necessary/necesario	dictionary/diccionario
7. -ty	Words ending with -ty in English, change to -tad ending in Spanish.	activity/actividad	difficulty/dificultad
8. -ion	Words ending with -ion, change to -ción, -sión.	nation/nación	addition/adición, division/division, education/educación
9. -ic, -ical	Words ending with -ic in English change -ico, -ica, -eco, -eca, in Spanish. Words ending with -ical change to -ico, -ica.	intrinsic/intrínseco, medical/médico	Catholic/Católico

	Rule	Examples	
10. - ment, -ant, -ent	Words ending in -*ment* change to –*mento*. Words ending in -*ant* change to –*ante*. Words ending in -*ent* change to –*ente*.	experiment/experimento instant/instante different/diferente	apartment/apartamento, president/presidente
11. -ence, -ance	Words ending in -*ence* change to –*encia*. Words ending in -*ance* change to –*ancia*.	influence/influencia, importance/importancia	difference/diferencia, silence/ silencio
12. -ure	Words ending in -*ure* change to -*ura*, -*uro*.	adventure/aventura	future/futuro
13. -ous	Words ending in -*ous* change to -*oso*, -*osa*.	famous/famoso	religious/religioso
14. -ive	Words ending in -*ive* change to -*ivo*, -*iva*.	active/activo	positive/positivo
15. -y	Words ending in -*y* change to -*ia*, -*io*.	family/familia	history/historia
16. -ly	Words ending in -*ly* change to -*mente*.	finally/finalmente	really/realmente
17. -ing	Words ending in -*ing* change to -*ando*, -*endo*, -*iendo*.	passing/ pasando	interesting/interesando
18. -ed	Words ending in -*ed* change to -*ado*, -*ido*.	accepted/aceptado decided/decidido	divided/dividido, entered/entrado
19. Infinitives	English verbs transform to Spanish by adding -*ar*, - *er*, -*ir* ending.	to cost/costar to move/mover to decide/decidir	explain/explicar, pass/pasar, serve/servir
20. Es (beginning)	Words *beginning* with *s*- in English change to *es*- in Spanish.	student/estudiante	slave/esclavo, stomach/estómago
21. Other	Variety of spelling differences.	coffee/café benefit/beneficio	baby/bebé, cent/centavo

FIGURE 6. 2. Catch a Cognate Cue Card

Cognates are words that look or sound alike in two languages and mean nearly the same thing. There are many Spanish/English cognates. When you learn how to *catch cognates* you will understand a lot of new words in English.

Directions

Look and Listen: Look at the new English word. Does it look like a word you know in Spanish? Read it aloud. Does it sound like a word you know in Spanish?

Think About It: Think about the meaning of the Spanish word that sounds most like the word in English.

Try It Out: Try using the Spanish word instead of the new English word in the sentence.

Check It Out: Does the Spanish word make sense in the sentence?

Celebrate! You've caught a cognate and learned a new word!

Note. From *Getting into words: Vocabulary instruction that strengthens comprehension* (p. 160), by S. Lubliner, ©2005, Baltimore, MD: Paul H. Brookes Publishing Co., Inc. Reprinted by permission.

Sample Lesson on Using the Catch a Cognate Cue Card: Ms. Carter

We observed Ms. Carter, a bilingual teacher, as she introduced the Catch a Cognate Cue Card. Ms. Carter said, "Look at the Catch a Cognate Cue Card on the overhead. Can you tell what I'm drawing? Yes, it's a fish. I want you to remember that catching cognates is like fishing. The more you catch, the more you eat [the children laughed]. What I really mean is that the more cognates you catch, the more words you'll learn in English."

Ms. Carter invited the children to read aloud each part of the cue card and she provided an example. Then she modeled the entire process with the word *organized* that appeared in the first paragraph of the social studies textbook. She began with Look and Listen, asking the students to look carefully at the word and to listen to the sound of the word as she read it aloud. Ms. Carter drew a picture of a brain on the overhead and asked the students to Think About It—and to decide what word in Spanish sounds the most like *organized*. Several students responded with the correct Spanish cognate, *organizado*. Then Ms. Carter called on a student to Try It Out—to read the sentence from the book and insert the Spanish word *organizado* instead of *organized*. She asked the students to explain the meaning of *organized* in their own words. Students offered suggestions as to the meaning of the word, coming up with definitions such as "fixed," "put together," and

FIGURE 6.3. Guidelines for Cognate Strategy Instruction

Provide rationale: Why are cognates important? One third to one half of all academic words are cognates so the cognate strategy will help you learn many words, comprehend better, and do better in school.

Introduce strategy: Use inductive activities to encourage student engagement; encourage students to hunt for cognates.

Explicit instruction: Explicitly teach each pattern, encouraging the students to look and listen for similarities and differences between the Spanish/English cognate pairs.

Model: Think aloud, demonstrating the use of the cognate strategy with each pattern.

Provide scaffolding: Provide the students with the Catch a Cognate Cue Card and coach them as they begin to use the cognate strategy.

Teach for transfer: Move cognate activities from worksheet to text.

Encourage collaboration: Provide opportunities for the students to work collaboratively on cognate activities.

Release responsibility: Encourage the students to internalize the cognate strategy and use it independently every time they read an English text.

"made nice." The students and teacher finally agreed on the definition "placed in order." Then Ms. Carter asked the students to Check It Out and the students agreed—it *does* make sense. Ms. Carter exclaimed enthusiastically, "We did it! We caught a cognate—now let's catch some more."

The lesson continued with students working with partners, using the Catch a Cognate Cue Card, and finding many more cognates in their social studies textbook. At the end of the lesson Ms. Carter asked the students to share the cognates they found and to summarize the meaning of the text in their own words.

Follow-up to Cognate Strategy Instruction Lessons

When we met with the teachers a few weeks later, it was clear that a major change had occurred as a result of the CSI lessons. Everyone agreed that the children loved the cognate instruction. The teachers reported that their students participated eagerly in the cognate lessons and appeared to relish the opportunity to be "experts." This was particularly notable with children who spoke very limited English and had rarely participated in class discussion before. Ms. Carter (the bilingual teacher) reported, "You know it was the first time that Juan ever spoke in class. He just got here from Mexico and he doesn't understand what is going on unless I explain it in Spanish. But when I taught the cognates he was smiling and raising his hand all the time."

The teachers' comments were confirmed when we visited the classes to talk to the students. They were eager to share their experiences. They found cognates everywhere, in a variety of subject areas, and pointed them out to their teachers and to their classmates. One of the students showed us her reading anthology, pointing out cognates she had found in the story she was reading.

The monolingual teachers' anxiety had abated by this point (midway through the project), but they needed additional support to feel confident in their ability to guide the students in recognizing cognates in the social studies textbook. In response to their requests, Lubliner provided the teachers with additional materials, highlighting cognates that appeared on each page of the social studies textbook. Figure 6.4 includes an example of a passage from the fifth-grade social studies textbook and the cognate list used for staff development (Porter et al., 2007, p. 226). When we shared this material, the teachers were quite surprised to see how many cognates this short passage contained.

EVALUATING THE EFFECTIVENESS OF COGNATE STRATEGY INSTRUCTION

Due to time constraints, the teachers taught 10 of 20 cognate lessons in the teacher's guide during the 11 weeks of the study. We examined the effectiveness of CSI instruction with a series of five tests that Lubliner developed. Teachers administered parallel versions of assessments before and after the cognate lessons. Figure 6.5 shows sample questions and answers from the tests.

The cognate tests were designed to assess students' ability to recognize cognates, understand vocabulary, and use cognate information in reading comprehension tasks. We began by comparing the pretest and posttest scores of students in each CSI class. The bilingual teacher's (Ms. Carter) class earned the highest scores on the Cognates in Context test. This seems logical, as she was most able to recognize cognates in a natural text herself. Ms. Carter's Spanish proficiency probably provided the students with more modeling of cognate awareness skills than the monolingual teachers could provide. But the students in Ms. Baker's (monolingual teacher) class outscored the other two classes on all of the other tests. This may be attributed to greater in-

FIGURE 6.4. Social Studies Textbook Excerpt and Cognate List

Colonial Trade

As a result of the many ships built in New England, trading became the center of the region's economy. The English government set up strict rules for trade. The government insisted that the colonists send their exports, or products leaving a country, only to England or to other English colonies. The government expected the colonists to buy only English-made imports, or goods brought into a country.

Trading ships leaving New England carried furs, lumber, grain, whale oil, and dried fish to England. The ships then returned to New England with tea, spices, and wine, as well as English-made goods, such as cloth, shoes, and paper.

Some colonial trading ships made even longer ocean voyages. They followed what became known as the triangular trade routes. These routes connected England, the English colonies, and Africa On a map, the routes formed triangles across the Atlantic Ocean.

Trading ships carried goods from England and raw materials from the English colonies and the West Indies. The ships also carried people who were captured from Central and Western Africa to become slaves. These people were sold as enslaved workers in the English colonies. During this time, millions of enslaved Africans were forced to travel across the Atlantic Ocean from Africa to the West Indies. This long ocean journey was called the Middle Passage.

colonial/colonial
result/resultado
New England/Nueva Inglaterra
center/centro
region/región
economy/economía
English/inglés
government/gobierno
strict/estricto
insisted/insistido
colonialists/colonialistas
exports/exportaciones
products/productos
England/Inglaterra
colonies/colonias
grain/grano
tea/té

spices/especias
wine/vino
ocean/océano
triangular/triangular
routes/rutas
connected/conectado
Africa/Africa
map/mapa
triangles/triángulos
Atlantic/atlántico
materials/materias
captured/capturado
central/central
slaves/esclavos, enslaved/esclavizó,
millions/millón,
forced/forzado,
middle passage/pasaje mediano

Note. Text pages from Harcourt Social Studies Textbook (Teacher's Edition, p. 226), by P. Porter et al., 2007, Orlando, FL. Reprinted with permission.

FIGURE 6.5. Sample Questions from CSI Assessment

1. Cognates in Isolation (students underlined cognates from a list of 100 words)
   republic
   <u>enough</u>
   <u>election</u>
   meaning
   fairness

2. Cognates in Context (students underlined cognates in a natural text)
   The Gonzales <u>family</u> traveled from <u>Mexico</u> to the <u>United States</u> by <u>train.</u> This trip was very <u>difficult.</u>

3. Comprehension (students answered multiple-choice comprehension questions based on the same text used to assess Cognates in Context)
   How did the family travel?
   > By ship
   > By plane
   > On foot
   > <u>By train</u>

4. Cloze (students inserted the appropriate words into a cognate-laden text)
   My grandparents _____ to the _____ from Europe in 1917. They left to escape _____ and to find _____ freedom.
   (immigrated, United States, poverty, religious)

5. Vocabulary (students selected definitions of cognates on a multiple-choice test).
   > opinion
   > <u>belief</u>
   > job
   > machine
   > vegetable

structional effectiveness on the part of Ms. Baker, though the principal and reading specialist considered all three teachers equally skilled. We wondered if this could have resulted from Ms. Baker's willingness to let her Spanish-speaking students be the "experts" in her class. These results are quite encouraging because they suggest that bilingualism is not a prerequisite for effective cognate strategy instruction.

We also compared the students' posttest results (all three CSI classes) with those of a fifth-grade class at the same school that did not receive the cognate instruction. When preexisting differences between classes were controlled (California Standards Test scores were used as a covariate), the students who received the cognate instruction outscored the other group on four out of five posttests, including Cognates in Isolation, Comprehension, Cloze, and Vocabulary. The differences were statistically significant and there were large effects favoring the group that received the cognate instruction.

DISCUSSION AND IMPLICATIONS

The results of the study suggest that CSI provides a promising instructional method and intervention tool for teachers with large numbers of Spanish-speaking bilingual students (see also Manyak, 2010). The teachers who worked with us on the Cognate Project also reported that the small number of monolingual English-speaking students in their classes acquired greater morphological awareness (awareness of word parts) and learned a large number of Latin-based roots and word families.

All three teachers deemed the lessons focused on cognate identification and the cognate strategy as the most useful components of the program. The teachers recognized the utility of teaching cognates in promoting students' English vocabulary, while fostering skills in the derivational relations stage of spelling. It is particularly important to note that the focus on Latin roots and related word families was effective in expanding the vocabulary of ELLs and English-only students alike. Knowledge of roots helps students understand a wide range of academic vocabulary, organized into extended word families. For example, learning the Latin root *man-*, meaning "hand," enables students to understand words such as *manuscript, manumission, manifest,* and *manual*. As Bear, Invernizzi, and Johnston, (2000) state, "Words that are related in meaning are often related in spelling as well, despite changes in sound" (p. 251). We suggest *Words Their Way with English Learners* (Bear, Helman, Templeton, Invernizzi, & Johnston, 2007) as a resource, since it contains examples of cognates, ready for instruction.

Our postproject interviews with the teachers led us to the conclusion that CSI was quite beneficial to them. The teachers reported that they learned to use cognates to teach word analysis in English and to expand students' academic vocabulary. The monolingual teachers reported learning much from their Spanish-speaking students in an exchange that resembles closely the "instructional conversations" first noted by Tharp and Gallimore (1991) and confirmed by subsequent research (e.g., see Many, 2002). We were heartened by teachers' willingness to allow their Spanish-speaking students to play the role of the expert in the classroom. Students' high level of engagement came as a distinctly pleasant finding for everyone involved in the project.

We suggest that teacher preparation programs include cognate instruction in their literacy methods courses, preparing beginning teachers to take advantage of the funds of knowledge Spanish-speaking students bring to school (Moll, Amanti, Neff, & Gonzalez, 1992). Both of us have included CSI in literacy courses we teach at our large public university, and have found that our students often remark on the utility and versatility of the strategy. Veteran teachers in the study echoed this judgment. We believe the process of sensitizing teachers to a new way of looking at language is critically important. When we began working on CSI, we became more sensitized to the power of the cognate strategy ourselves. Lubliner is bilingual, while Grisham has some background in Spanish, but we found that you don't need a great deal of fluency in Spanish to identify cognates. Now we, too, look for cognates whenever we read.

We plan to continue our work with Cognate Strategy Instruction, with the goal of increasing the transferability of the strategy to content areas other than social studies. Our ongoing work involves helping teachers develop their own CSI lessons based on their own curriculum, rather than relying on structured lessons that we provide. We are hopeful that future studies will demonstrate an increased effect of CSI as teachers and students become more familiar with cognate patterns and increasingly adept at applying the strategy to improve their understanding of complex academic texts.

REFERENCES

Bear, D. R., Helman, L., Invernizzi, M., Templeton, S., & Johnston, F. (2007). *Words their way with English learners: Word study for phonics, vocabulary, and spelling instruction.* Upper Saddle River, NJ: Pearson.

Bear, D. R., Invernizzi, M., & Johnston, F. (2000). *Words their way: Word study for phonics, vocabulary, and spelling instruction* (2nd ed.). Upper Saddle River, NJ: Merrill.

Bereiter, C., & Bird, M. (1985). Use of thinking aloud in identification and teaching of reading comprehension strategies. *Cognition and Instruction, 2*(2), 131–156.

Bravo, M., Hiebert, E., & Pearson, D. (2005). Tapping the linguistic resources of Spanish/English bilinguals: The role of cognates in science. In R. K. Wagner,

A. Muse, & K. Tannenbaum (Eds.), *Vocabulary acquisition: Implications for reading comprehension* (pp. 140–156). New York, NY: Guilford Press.

Brown, A. (1985). *Teaching students to think as they read: Implications for curriculum reform* (Reading Education Report No. 58). Champaign: University of Illinois at Urbana-Champaign, Center for the Study of Reading.

Brown, A., & Palinscar, A. (1986). *Guided cooperative learning and individual knowledge acquisition.* (Technical Report No. 372). Washington, DC: U.S. Department of Education.

Chall, J. S., Jacobs, V. A., & Baldwin, L. E. (1990). *Reading crisis: Why poor children fall behind.* Cambridge, MA: Harvard University Press.

Coxhead, A. (2000). A new academic word list. *TESOL Quarterly, 34,* 213–238. Retrieved from http://www.jstor.org/stable/3587951

Dole, J., Brown, K., & Trathen, W. (1996). The effects of strategy instruction on the comprehension performance of at-risk students. *Reading Research Quarterly, 31*(1), 62–88.

García, G. (1999). Bilingual children's reading: An overview of recent research. *CAL Resources Archive, 23*(1).

Hiebert, E. H., & Lubliner, S. (2008). The nature, learning, and instruction of general academic vocabulary. In A. Farstrup & S. J. Samuels (Eds.), *What research has to say about vocabulary instruction* (pp. 106–129). Newark, DE: International Reading Association.

Jepsen, C., & Alth, S. (2005). *English learners in California schools.* San Francisco: Public Policy Institute of California.

Jimenez, R. T., García, G. E., & Pearson, P. D. (1996). The reading strategies of bilingual Latina/o students who are successful English readers: Opportunities and obstacles. *Reading Research Quarterly, 31,* 90–112.

Lubliner, S. (2005). *Getting into words: Vocabulary instruction that strengthens comprehension.* Baltimore, MD: Brookes.

Lubliner, S., & Hiebert, E. (2011). An analysis of English-Spanish cognates as a source of general academic language, *Bilingual Research Journal, 34*(1).

Many, J. (2002). An exhibition and analysis of verbal tapestries: Understanding how scaffolding is woven into the fabric of instructional conversations. *Reading Research Quarterly, 37*(4), 376–407.

Manyak, P. C. (2010). Vocabulary instruction for English learners: Lessons from MCVIP. *The Reading Teacher, 64*(2), 143–146.

Moll, L., Amanti, C., Neff, D., & Gonzalez, N. (1992). Funds of knowledge for teaching: Using a qualitative approach to connect homes and classrooms. *Theory Into Practice, 31,* 132–141.

Montelongo, J. A., Hernandez, A. C., & Herter, R. J. (2009). Orthographic transparency and morphology of Spanish-English cognate adjectives. *Psychological Reports, 105,* 970–974.

Nagy, W. (1986). *The influence of word and text properties on learning from context* (Technical Report No. 369). Urbana, IL: Illinois University, Center for the Study of Reading.

Nagy, W., García, G., Durgunolu, A., & Hancin-Bhatt, B. (1993). Spanish-English bilingual children's use and recognition of cognates in English reading. *Journal of Reading Behavior, 25,* 241–259.

Nagy, W., Herman, P., & Anderson, R. (1985). Learning words from context. *Reading Research Quarterly, 20,* 233–253.

Nash, R. (1997). *NTC's dictionary of Spanish cognates.* Chicago, IL: NTC Publishing Group.

National Center for Education Statistics (NCES). (2009). *Nation's Report Card: Reading 2009.* Retrieved from http://nces.ed.gov/pubsearch/pubsinfo. asp?pubid=2010458

Palincsar, A. (1983*). Reciprocal teaching of comprehension-monitoring activities* (Report No. US-NIE-C-400-76-0116). Washington, DC: U.S. Department of Education.

Palincsar, A. (1984). *Reciprocal teaching: Working within the zone of proximal development.* Paper presented at the annual meeting of the American Educational Research Association, New Orleans, LA.

Palincsar, A. (1985). *The unpacking of a multi-component, metacognitive training package.* Paper presented at the annual meeting of the American Educational Research Association, Chicago, IL.

Palincsar, A. (1986). The role of dialogue in providing scaffolded instruction. *Educational Psychologist, 21*(1 &2), 73–98.

Palincsar, A. S., & Brown, A. L. (1985). Reciprocal teaching: A means to a meaningful end. In J. Osborn, P. Wilson, & R. C. Anderson (Eds.) *Reading Education: Foundations for a Literate America* (pp. 2199–2310). Lexington, MA: Lexington Books.

Porter, P., Berson, M., Hill, M., Howard, T., Larson, B., & Moreno, J. (2007). *Reflections: The United States: Making a new nation.* Orlando, FL: Harcourt.

Proctor, C. P., Dalton, B., & Grisham, D. L. (2007). Scaffolding English language learners and struggling readers in a universal literacy environment with embedded strategy instruction and vocabulary support. *Journal of Literacy Research, 39*(1), 71–93.

Proctor, C. P., & Mo, E. (2009). The relationship between cognate awareness and English comprehension among Spanish-English bilingual fourth grade students. *TESOL Quarterly, 43*(1), 126–136.

Stanovich, K. (1986). Matthew effects in reading: Some consequences of individual differences in the acquisition of literacy. *Reading Research Quarterly, 21*(4), 360–406.

Tabors, P., Páez, M., & López, L. (2003). Dual language abilities of four-year olds: Initial findings from the early childhood study of language and literacy development of Spanish-speaking children. *NABE Journal of Research and Practice, 1*(1), 70–91.

Tharp, R. G., & Gallimore, R. (1991). *The instructional conversation: Teaching and learning in social activity* (Research Report: 2). Washington, DC: National Center for Research on Cultural Diversity and Second Language Learning. (ERIC Reproduction Document No. ED341254)

Weinstein, C., & Mayer, R. (1986). The teaching of learning strategies. In M. Wittrock (Ed.), *Handbook of research on teaching* (3rd ed., pp. 315–327). New York, NY: Macmillan.

CHAPTER 7

"What I Know About Spanish Is That I Don't Talk It Much"

Bilingual Fifth-Grade Students' Perceptions of Bilingualism

Sandra A. Butvilofsky

No toda mi familia sabe dos idiomas. Yo soy una de las afortunadas que sabe dos idiomas. Saber dos idiomas me ha ayudado a conseguir muchas cosas. . . . Una vez yo y mi mamá fuimos a la tienda y necesitabamos una medicina pa mi hermana. Pero la señora que estaba allí no sabía español y mi mamá tampoco sabía ingles. . . . Si yo no hablara dos idiomas nosotros no hubieramos conseguido lo que queriamos.

[Not everyone in my family knows two languages. I am fortunate to know two languages. Knowing two languages has helped me do many things. . . . Once, my mom and I went to the store to get some medicine for my sister. But the woman that worked there did not know Spanish and my mom didn't know English. . . . If I didn't speak two languages we wouldn't have gotten what we needed.]

—Flor

This excerpt from a fifth-grade bilingual student's writing reflects one of the many functions bilingualism serves, as identified by Spanish-and-English-speaking Latino students participating in a biliteracy research project. In this instance, the possession of two languages by Flor (a pseudonym, as are all names of participants and schools in the study) serves as a positive attribute of her identity as she considers herself fortunate to know two languages, and Flor's ability to

124

alternate between both languages allowed her family to get what they needed to help her sister. Flor's cognizance of the value of bilingualism is evident. Unfortunately, not all of the emerging bilingual students represented in this particular study acknowledged their bilingualism or the many benefits of knowing two languages (I sometimes replace the term *English language learners* (ELLs) with the term *emerging bilingual students* because it acknowledges the dynamic process of acquiring two languages rather than focusing solely on the acquisition of the English language). This lack of acknowledgment can be attributed to emerging bilingual students' internalization of the external political and ideological pressures for assimilation toward monolingualism, which oftentimes thwarts the development of bilingualism and biliteracy.

Emerging bilinguals make up the fastest growing population of students attending public schools in large urban districts in the United States today (Genesee, Lindholm-Leary, Saunders, & Christian, 2005), however, only 20% of them are in some type of program that promotes and develops their bilingualism (Zehler et al., 2003). Despite the fact that the academic benefits of bilingual education programs have been established and documented within the United States (August & Hakuta, 1997; Ramírez, Pasta, Yuen, & Ramey, 1991; Thomas & Collier, 1997), bilingualism is a highly contested political issue in the realm of public education for certain groups of students, and biliteracy is rarely referenced. Decisions as to who is entitled to bilingualism are paradoxical. This paradox manifests itself in the various stances taken toward language diversity, which are exemplified in education policies. Some policies, like the No Child Left Behind Act, encourage the teaching of foreign languages to students to increase "national security and global competitiveness," while other policies forbid the use of any language other than English, especially for minority language students or ELLs. Since 1988, voters in California, Arizona, and Massachusetts have approved ballot initiatives restricting bilingual education in those states. Initiatives and accountability measures that force emerging bilingual students into English-only instruction limit emerging bilingual students' full linguistic and literate potential.

In this chapter I use emerging bilingual students' voices to support my argument that more must be done to ensure that bilingualism and biliteracy are supported and maintained in bilingual education programs. Often the primary function of developing bilingualism in Spanish-and-English-speaking children living in the United States is only understood to serve as a temporary medium of instruction. That is, once students have developed a certain level of proficiency in English that enables them to receive instruction primarily in English, there is little regard for maintaining their bilingualism. However, as illustrated above in Flor's writing, for many bilingual students, the function of bilingualism exists far beyond the classroom walls. Bilingualism and biliteracy are not only advantageous for the students but also for their communities, as bilingualism and biliteracy provide cognitive benefits not available to monolingual and monoliterate children (Moll & Dworin, 1996).

The purpose of this chapter, therefore, is to present the seldom-acknowledged perceptions of emerging bilingual students' experiences as they develop their bilingualism and biliteracy in a biliteracy program. This inquiry provides a different perspective of the functions of bilingualism, as the perspectives come directly from students and therefore puts "children in the center stage in the world as they see it" (Dyson, 1997, p. 9). Through their writing, fifth-grade Latino students describe both the benefits and struggles of learning and maintaining two languages. They bring to light the often-neglected emotional and psychological aspects they experience, as they have to navigate two cultural worlds while learning two languages. The findings from this study illuminate the many functions of bilingualism as identified by bilingual fifth-grade students, and at the same time, students reveal their awareness of the asymmetric relationship between Spanish and English in the United States.

By attending to and understanding students' perspectives, it is my intention, through the voice of emerging bilingual students participating in a biliteracy program, to share and promote the value of developing bilingualism and biliteracy. Through these writing samples, educators, researchers, and policy makers have a unique opportunity to learn firsthand how students who participate in bilingual education programs feel about their experience as they learned two languages and literacies. This chapter reinforces the importance of recognizing the intersection of literacy research that is situated in multiple-language contexts and the critical roles language and literacy development play in the lived experiences of emerging bilingual students. The questions addressed in this chapter are these: What do students say they are doing with their Spanish and English through their writing samples? And how do students perceive the relationship between Spanish and English, as illustrated in their writing?

A SOCIOLINGUISTIC PERSPECTIVE

A sociolinguistic theory of bilingualism provides the framework for understanding how students perceive and use their bilingualism. Sociolinguistics stresses the social nature of language and its use in varying contexts, assuming that "language is not only cognitive but also cultural, social, and situated" (Moschkovich, 2006, p. 122). As such, a bilingual individual's choice in language use is not only influenced by the individual's own attitude or preference toward a certain language, but also by the relative status of the languages within various contexts (Baker, 2001; Coulmas, 2005). Accordingly, sociolinguists attribute language choice to three conditions: with whom the individual is speaking, where the individual is located, and when the interaction is occurring (Fishman, 1965). In other words, the framework for this chapter resides in the notion that an individual's possession of two languages (Mackey, 1962/2000; Wei, 2000) is "the product of a specific linguistic community that uses one of its languages for certain functions and the other for other functions or situations" (Moschkovich, 2006, p. 123).

In addition, sociolinguists are interested in seeing how the language repertoire of bilinguals may change over time (Grosjean, 1998). Changes in the competency of skills between languages may occur as the environment changes or as an awareness of the value and status given to the two languages is understood (Escamilla, 1994; Grosjean, 1989, 2008). This is especially true when the majority group does not have a great level of tolerance for the minority group and its language. This intolerance toward language diversity has been manifested in English-only movements that have dismantled bilingual education in various areas in the United States. The asymmetric relationship between languages may put linguistic minorities under pressure to adopt the majority language and often leads to language shift or loss within three generations (Coulmas, 2005; Fillmore, 1991).

In bilingual education, empirical studies using a sociolinguistic framework have described the status and function of two languages in contact with one another according to the context (Escamilla, 1994; McCollum, 1999; Reyes, 2004). Through sociolinguistic theory, researchers have demonstrated how the status of a language in a multilinguistic context has the capacity to influence a bilingual's choice in language use. Sociolinguistic studies have demonstrated how the status of a language can affect the goals of programs attempting to develop bilingualism and biliteracy (Fitts, 2006). The study that this chapter covers uses a sociolinguistic framework in order to understand students' perceptions of their bilingualism and biliteracy. This framework acknowledges that emerging bilingual students' use of linguistic, literacy, and cultural resources are influenced by situated sociocultural, sociohistorical, and sociopolitical factors.

CONTEXT FOR THE STUDY:
INTRODUCTION TO LITERACY SQUARED®

The students represented herein were part of a larger biliteracy program and research project called Literacy Squared®, in which Spanish and English literacy instruction was provided and maintained from first through fifth grade. The biliteracy program and research project was created to serve Spanish-and-English-speaking bilingual students in transitional bilingual programs (Escamilla & Hopewell, 2010). Literacy Squared® was purposefully designed utilizing theories of bilingualism in which a bilingual individual's languages are not seen as separate entities within the individual, but rather as part of a whole, having the capacity to influence and interact with one another (Grosjean, 1989; Valdés & Figueroa, 1994). Literacy Squared® subscribes to a holistic theory of bilingualism that acknowledges and capitalizes upon the full linguistic repertoire of the bilingual individual.

Literacy Squared® is an innovative approach to literacy teaching for Spanish-speaking students attending urban schools with high percentages of Latinos and the majority of students receiving free or reduced-price lunch. First conceived in 2004, the program and research purpose was twofold: (1) to examine the potential in providing paired literacy instruction in both Spanish and English starting in first grade and continuing through fifth grade, and (2) to develop new paradigms and theories regarding the biliteracy development of Spanish/English bilingual students (Escamilla & Hopewell, 2010). Unlike other bilingual programs, Literacy Squared ensures that English literacy instruction is not witheld until a minimal threshold is achieved in Spanish literacy and/or oral English proficiency. Rather, students receive literacy-based English as a second language (ESL) beginning in first grade, alongside Spanish literacy instruction.

Paired literacy instruction has been recommended as a promising practice for ELLs in several recent research syntheses (August & Shanahan, 2006; Slavin & Cheung, 2003). Specific time allocations for Spanish literacy and literacy-based ESL are designated by grade level. Literacy-based ESL considers what children already know about reading and writing in Spanish and how to apply those skills and strategies in English while also focusing on instruction in ESL. Some of the key components of literacy-based ESL include the use of appropriately leveled and culturally relevant texts; explicit and direct instruction of English literacy skills and strategies that utilize explicit cross-language connections; and a focus on oracy, which is intended to help children develop the language necessary for success in reading and writing. In addition, Literacy Squared continues the practice of providing literacy instruction in Spanish and English through fifth grade, whereas traditional bilingual programs stop the use of native language instruction, thus limiting literacy instruction to only English around third grade.

One of the main constructs of Literacy Squared involved the creation of a trajectory toward biliteracy. Literacy Squared recognizes that when emerging bilingual children are instructed simultaneously in Spanish literacy and literacy-based ESL, they will develop literacy in both languages, though the development of each language will not be equivalent. Rather, it was hypothesized that emerging bilingual children's literacy development in Spanish would be slightly more advanced than their English literacy, but a large discrepancy would not exist between the two. This staggered leveling of biliteracy development is referred to as the "zone of scaffolded biliteracy" (Escamilla & Hopewell, 2010). In other words, student achievement in one language has a direct and measurable correspondence in the second language.

Longitudinal findings for cohorts of students participating in the Literacy Squared research project demonstrated positive gains in Spanish and English reading and writing (Escamilla & Hopewell, 2010; Sparrow, Butvilofsky, & Escamilla, 2012). Findings indicate that the longer students receive paired literacy instruction, the more likely they are to be reading and writing comparably in both languages. While the difference between Spanish and English reading scores appears to be greater in first grade, as students progress through the intervention, the difference between Spanish and English reading achievement decreases. In other words, emerging bilingual children are on a positive trajectory toward developing biliteracy.

WRITING SAMPLES FOR STUDY ON STUDENT PERSPECTIVES

Data examined for this particular study included Spanish and English writing samples from 79 fifth-grade students in six schools participating in the Literacy Squared project, which were collected during the 2007–08 school year, the first year in which fifth-grade data were collected. Spanish and English writing samples were collected annually as part of the research project, and in fifth grade, students were asked to reflect on their bilingualism in response to a prompt. All 79 students included in this particular study are Latino, were classified as ELLs, and qualified for free or reduced priced lunch, which generally serves as a proxy for socioeconomic status.

Spanish and English writing data are collected yearly from all participants in the Literacy Squared intervention. Students are asked to write to similar prompts in Spanish and English for 30 minutes. Similarity in prompts was used to elicit cross-language transfer, yet sameness was avoided so as to not encourage translation. The fifth-grade writing prompts were as follows:

Spanish: *Piensa en tu vida personal y escolar, ¿Cómo te ha ayudado saber dos idiomas?* [Think about your personal and school lives. How has knowing two languages helped you in school and in your personal life?]

English: Think about your experiences learning Spanish and English. What is hard? What is easy?

Using a sociolinguistic perspective, each student's Spanish and English writing samples were read through, analyzed, and coded. Because language is social and "cannot be defined without reference to its speakers and the context of its use" (Wei, 2000, p. 12), all writing samples were analyzed to identify *which* language was used, with *whom*, and *where* or in which context (Fishman, 1965; Grosjean, 2008). Students cited using Spanish and/or English with family members (parents, grandparents, siblings, cousins, and other extended family), teachers, friends/classmates and others (which included people outside of the school or home context). The number of times a student mentioned using Spanish or English with one of the aforementioned persons was tallied. Codes were also created to account for the context (home, school, and other); and the frequency with which a student wrote about using either language in a specific context was also calculated. An additional analysis was conducted to account for the students' awareness of the asymmetrical relationship between Spanish and English.

FUNCTIONS OF BILINGUALISM

Using a sociolinguistic perspective, three main functions describing the students' perceived uses of and purposes for bilingualism emerged

from their Spanish and English writing samples: communication, brokering, and cultural advantage. Collectively, these themes yield an understanding of what students actually do with their bilingualism and
what they perceive as advantageous in knowing two languages.

Communication

> *A mi me ha ayudado mucho aprender 2 idiomas, porque ahora puedo*
> *comunicarme con otras personas. Por ejemplo si yo conozco a alguien*
> *que no he visto en mi vida y esa persona hable ingles yo le podría*
> *preguntar lo que quisiera. Pero si yo no pudiera hablar el ingles yo no le*
> *pudiera hablar.*

> [Learning two languages has helped me, because now I can
> communicate with others. For example if I meet someone I have
> never seen in my life and that person speaks English I would
> be able to ask whatever I want. But if I didn't know English I
> wouldn't be able to speak with him.] (Jasmín)

Being understood by others, understanding others, and communicating with others in Spanish and English was the overarching function of bilingualism. This finding is consistent with the social function
of language, which is to communicate (Wei, 2000). As reflected in
Jasmín's excerpt above, speaking two languages created opportunities
to interact with others in the wider community. The communicative
function of language was not only related to individuals, but also to
various media sources such as television, movies, and different printed
material.

While students wrote about the benefits of being bilingual, they
also wrote about the difficulties of learning English. They expressed
feelings of frustration, shame, and sadness, especially within the classroom.

> When I came to school the teacher use to talk to me an [in]
> english. Put a [I] diden understand her she would get mad at
> me . . . they wold tell me to do someting and I still thent [didn't]
> getet [get it] then I got in trobul. (Jaime)

Despite the teacher's repetition of the directions, Jaime could not understand, and as a result of his inability to understand English, he was
not only punished by the teacher, but he was also foreclosed from
meaningfully participating in learning.

Learning was so hard because ebery botty [k]new English etsept [except] me . . . wen we read in grups the teacher maked me read but I was anberest [embarrassed] because I dirent [k]now anyting or how to read soo I cried. (Jaime)

While students may not always externalize their struggles, having an awareness of them can help teachers affirm and acknowledge students' experiences as they become bilingual. Furthermore, if these students, most of whom had the opportunity to use their native language, experienced such emotional stress, imagine what happens to the majority of emerging bilingual children who are in English-only contexts and are not afforded the opportunity to use their native language in school.

Brokering

I have to use my english sometimes to translate what english people are saying, because my family talks mostly Spanish. (Amelia)

Many students wrote about *brokering*, or using Spanish and English to translate for family or friends in the wider community, school, or home. As defined by Tse (1996), *brokering* is "interpretations and translation performed in everyday situations by bilinguals who have no special training" (p. 486). In addition to translating, the following excerpt from José's writing demonstrates the important role his possession of two languages plays for his family.

Mi papa no abla en ingles y no les entiende a las personas. Por eso yo le ayudo a mi papá ablando dos idiomas. El siempre me yeva a donde necesita ayuda ablando ingles. Cuando no entiend[e] me dice a mi que able para el.

[My dad does not speak English and he does not understand other people. That's why I help him because I speak two languages. He always takes me when he needs me to speak English. When he doesn't understand he tells me to speak for him.] (José)

In the above excerpt, José is demonstrating the important role he plays for his father: José is his father's voice in a sense. This specific example demonstrates the complexity of some children's role in their family and their need to alternate between two languages for their survival and decision making.

Cultural Advantage

Sabiendo dos idiomas a mejorado mi vida. Cuando sea grande voy a tener mas oportunidades de trabajo.

[Knowing two languages has improved my life. When I grow up I will have more job opportunities.] (Victor)

Many students discussed the added macrosociolinguistic benefits of being in possession of two languages (Wei, 2000). These added benefits include better grades, potential economic benefits of having greater job opportunities, earning a higher income, attending college, developing relationships with and understanding people from different backgrounds and languages, and helping the wider community. Manuel writes:

Y yo se que sabiendo el inglés y el español me va a ayudar en el futuro para cuando vaya a trabajar. Estoy feliz de saber dos idiomas. También me puede ayudar en poderle enseñar a mi familia en ingles y el español a mis amigos que quieren aprender español. Al saber 2 idiomas puede que me ayude en tener una vida mejor y un mejor trabajo.

[I know that English and Spanish is going to help me when I work in the future. I am happy to know two languages. It can also help me teach my family Spanish and English and my friends that want to learn Spanish. Knowing two languages can help me have a better life and a better job.] (Manuel)

Not only is knowing two languages helpful for this student's future financial life, but he will also be able to teach his family English and his friends Spanish. Manuel's recognition of his bilingualism facilitates his agency in widening his choices for his own life, as well as affecting others around him by teaching them another language.

Another cultural advantage worth discussing, which is particularly pertinent to Literacy Squared, was the students' awareness of how knowing two languages provided them with academic advantages. The academic advantages did not only include access to better grades and the potential to go to college, but also an awareness that knowing two languages provided students the opportunity to participate in two literacy and cultural systems.

> *Todo me gusta de aprender dos lenguajes pero lo que me encanta mas es leer. Saber dos lenguajes me ayuda en mi lectura. Me deja tener la habilidad de poder leer cualquier libro de mi gusto aunque sea ingles ó español lo podria entender.*

> [I like everything about learning two languages but what most enchants me is reading. Knowing two languages helps me in my reading. It allows me the ability to read whichever book I like, whether it is in English or Spanish, I could understand it.] (Jasmín)

HEGEMONY OF ENGLISH

The students expressed much more about bilingualism than just its functions. Their writing reflected some of the unspoken realities of the asymmetrical relationship between Spanish and English in the United States. I say unspoken realities because the students did not explicitly write about the "unequal" relationship between the languages: instead, their writing reflected some of the subtle shifts individuals make in language choice when a majority and minority language are in contact with one another. The notion of losing proficiency in Spanish, choosing English over Spanish, and explicitly identifying with being bilingual explain some of the complex perceptions students in this study held about the relationship between Spanish and English.

When analyzing and recording with whom and in which contexts students used a particular language, it became evident that students used Spanish and English in separate contexts and with different individuals. Students used English in school with teachers, friends, and other students more than Spanish. Spanish was mostly used in the home with various family members. While students did write about using Spanish at school, the use of English was accounted for with more frequency. This finding is consistent with other research in bilingual education contexts in the United States, where English holds a higher status than Spanish (Escamilla, 1994; Fillmore, 1991; Gerena, 2010; McCollum, 1999). According to Wei (2000), "typically, multilingual societies tend to assign different roles to different languages; one language may be used in informal contexts with family and friends, while another for the more formal situations of work, education and government" (p. 13). The language used in more formal contexts is thus the language of higher status (Coulmas, 2005; Grosjean, 1985).

LANGUAGE SHIFT AND LOSS

Despite efforts to promote and develop biliteracy and bilingualism within Literacy Squared schools, hegemonic influences compel students' use of English over Spanish. Mention of language loss and/or language shift appeared in more than half of the writing samples. A writing sample was coded language loss or language shift when a student wrote about using English more than Spanish, their loss in Spanish proficiency, or their parents' concern over them not using Spanish. In the following excerpt taken from Maria's English writing sample, she mentions both her own choice of using English more often than Spanish and her mother's concern with language shift:

> What I know about Spanish is that I don't talk it much. I talk English most of the time. That's why at the dinner table my mom always says, *"hablen español,"* [speak Spanish] So I do. (Maria)

Maria's mother tells her to "speak Spanish" at the dinner table, thus showing her attempts to prevent Maria's language loss. In addition to students choosing to speak English more often than Spanish, the amount of time spent using English in school increases as well, which leads to an eventual increase in English proficiency and a decrease in Spanish proficiency as demonstrated in this statement:

> The sad part of using English in classes was that I was forgetting my Spanish. Spanish was getting harder and harder for me. (Carlos)

For some of the students, the shift toward English use over Spanish use was unintentional, as school, district, and state policies require students to take high-stakes assessments in English even though students are participating in bilingual programs. For Eddy, his preference for English can be attributed to his desire to pass his state's high-stakes test in English, the Texas Assessment of Knowledge and Skills (TAKS).

This year in fifth grade my only goals are to past the English TAKS. . . . I like more english than Spanish so I hope I can past the tests in English.

Although the students were aware of their choice in languages, they were also negotiating the maintenance of their Spanish within their homes with their parents or other family members. Take, for example, Daniel. Not only is he in a position to choose between languages, but he can now teach his mom English, while she helps him maintain his Spanish:

Mi mamá quiere aprender ingles. Yo le enseño y como se me olvida el español ella me enseña a mi.

[My mom wants to learn English. So I teach her and since I am forgetting Spanish, she teaches me.] (Daniel)

For some students, speaking Spanish in the home is not just a choice, but also a necessity as Yessenia explains:

Para mi hablar en español es muy importante porque mis padres ablan en español.

[Speaking Spanish is very important to me because my parents speak Spanish.] (Yessenia)

This necessity to preserve Spanish in order to communicate with family members is vital to maintaining and developing relationships. When families lose their ability to communicate with one another, "rifts develop and families lose the intimacy that comes from shared beliefs and understanding" (Fillmore, 1991, p. 343).

Even though many students expressed their preference for using English, a few students expressed their preference for speaking Spanish and were adamant about maintaining both their language and their culture:

I'm happy that I know 2 languages and I haven't forgotten about my Spanish culture and also thanks to my family and my mom I will always talk Spanish but I will never forget english either. (Liliana)

This sense of pride in possessing two languages was conveyed in several other samples and is addressed in students' identification of self as bilingual.

IDENTIFICATION OF SELF AS BILINGUAL

Although both the English and the Spanish writing prompts made explicit reference to the use of two languages (Spanish and English), not all of the students directly identified themselves as bilingual or in possession of two languages. When students acknowledged their bilingualism explicitly, they sometimes attached a statement of pride or honor to it. For example:

> *Yo estoy ogulloso de saber dos idiomas haci puedo enceñarle a mi hermanito y mis primitos.*

> [I am proud to know two languages so I can teach my little brother and my cousins.] (José)

Another interesting acknowledgement of bilingualism, made by Jessica, was the pride she experienced in knowing two languages although the school did not formally recognize her as being proficient academically in English as demonstrated by assessments.

> *Aunque abeses agarro malos grados porque ago los examenes en ingles yo stoy orgullosa de mi misma porque lla [ya] se otro idioma.*

> [Although I sometimes get bad grades because I take tests in English, I am proud of myself because I know another language.] (Jessica)

This excerpt from Jessica clearly shows that the possession of two languages has much more to do with one's identity or ability to communicate than just performing academic tasks in school.

CONCLUSION

The purpose of this study was to present and describe bilingual fifth-grade students' personal perceptions of bilingualism as related in their Spanish and English writing samples. Most studies concerning bilingual education programs focus on the cognitive and linguistic aspects of bilingual programs; however, this study highlights some of the emotional and psychological elements of students' experiences in their lives inside and outside school. Many students in this study understood and articulated the benefits of bilingualism. For them, Spanish did not only serve as a bridge to English, but bilingualism served a greater function and purpose. Some students illustrated that their possession of two languages serves as a navigational device in order to develop meaningful relationships, negotiate communication between persons and other media, and achieve both personal and financial security in multiple worlds. These functions of bilingualism emphasize the need for various communities, especially schools, to encourage and nurture the simultaneous development of both Spanish and English. In addition, schools should engage students in discussions about the advantages and needs for bilingualism.

Knowing and understanding students' perspectives and experiences are important as they can inform curriculum development, policies for emerging bilingual students, and reading and writing instruction. I believe that the findings related to students' perceptions of bilingualism can inform educational practices for emerging bilingual children.

If emerging bilingual children are to develop their bilingual and biliterate potential in bilingual programs, we must recognize the possession of two languages and the ability to navigate two cultural worlds and literacy systems as resources. I suggest the following guidelines for nurturing and legitimizing bilingualism and biliteracy:

1. Maintain formal reading and writing instruction in Spanish and English, starting as early as kindergarten and continuing through fifth grade and beyond.
2. Native language use must be legitimized within the classroom and the school, both in bilingual and in English-only programs. This can be accomplished by creating environments in which students are afforded the opportunity to use their native language for various purposes such as to express understanding, to read, and to write.
3. The benefits and challenges of being bilingual and biliterate should be discussed openly and directly. These discussions must address the emotional and psychological difficulty of having to learn another language. Just as important, it is necessary to discuss the macrosociolinguistic benefits of bilingualism.

4. Students should be given multiple opportunities to read books about bilingualism and books about others' experiences navigating two cultural worlds and linguistic systems.
5. School personnel should go out of their way to speak the minority language outside of the classroom to model the utility and worth of the language.
6. Parents need to be encouraged to continue nurturing the home language.

In conclusion, good bilingual and biliteracy programs should explicitly address all of the issues listed above by providing emerging bilingual students opportunities to read and write in two languages and actively discuss bilingualism. In addition, it is important for bilingual educators and researchers to include the voices and perspectives of bilingual students. Listening to bilingual students and understanding what they think about their languages has the potential to improve program development and, ultimately, promote emerging bilinguals' linguistic resources. It is difficult to really understand what we are teaching without asking students what it is they are learning. The questions we need to ask should go beyond asking about the content being taught, but how what it is we teach is affecting our emerging bilingual students and how what we teach may be useful to them outside of the school walls; as was expressed by many of the students in this inquiry, the functions of bilingualism and the potential in biliteracy development reach beyond the classroom and school context.

Acknowledgment. I wish to thank Kathy Escamilla and Olivia Ruiz-Figueroa for developing and actualizing the Literacy Squared biliteracy program and research project. Thanks to this project I was able to conduct this inquiry and write this chapter.

REFERENCES

August, D., & Hakuta, K. (1997). *Improving schooling for language minority students: A research agenda.* Washington, DC: National Academy Press.

August, D., & Shanahan, T. (2006). *Developing literacy in second-language learners: Report of the national literacy panel on language-minority children and youth.* Mahwah, NJ: Erlbaum.

Baker, C. (2001). *Foundations of bilingual education and bilingualism.* Clevedon, UK: Multilingual Matters.

Coulmas, F. (2005). *Sociolinguistics: The study of speakers' choices*. New York, NY: Cambridge University Press.

Dyson, A. H. (1997). *Writing superheroes: Contemporary childhood, popular culture, and classroom Literacy*. New York, NY: Teachers College Press.

Escamilla, K. (1994). The sociolinguistic environment of a bilingual school: A case study introduction. *Bilingual Research Journal, 18*, 21–47.

Escamilla, K., & Hopewell, S. (2010). Transitions to biliteracy: Creating positive academic trajectories for emerging bilinguals in the United States. In J. Petrovic (Ed.), *International perspectives on bilingual education: Policy, practice, and controversy* (pp. 69–93). Charlotte, NC: Information Age.

Fillmore, L. W. (1991). When learning a second language means losing the first. *Early Childhood Research Quarterly, 6*, 323–346.

Fishman, J. A. (1965). Who speaks what language to whom and when. *La Linguistique, 2*, 67–88.

Fitts, S. (2006). Reconstructing the status quo: Linguistic interaction in a dual-language school. *Bilingual Research Journal, 29*, 337–365.

Genesee, F., Lindholm-Leary, K., Saunders, W., & Christian, D. (2005). English language learners in U.S. schools: An overview of research findings. *Journal of Education for Students Placed At Risk, 10*(4), 363–385.

Gerena, L. (2010). Student attitudes toward biliteracy in dual immersion programs. *The Reading Matrix, 10*, 55–78.

Grosjean, F. (1985). The bilingual as a competent but specific speaker-hearer. *Journal of Multilingual and Multicultural Development, 6*, 467–477.

Grosjean, F. (1989). Neurolinguists, beware! The bilingual is not two monolinguals in one person. *Brain and Language, 36*, 3–15.

Grosjean, F. (1998). Studying bilinguals: Methodological and conceptual issues. *Bilingualism: Language and Cognition, 1*, 131–149.

Grosjean, F. (2008). *Studying bilinguals*. New York, NY: Oxford University Press.

Mackey, W. F. (2000). The description of bilingualism. In L. Wei (Ed.), *The bilingual reader*. London, UK: Routledge. (Reprinted from *Canadian Journal of Linguistics, 7*, 51– 85, in 1962)

McCollum, P. (1999). Learning to value English: Cultural capital in a two-way bilingual program. *Bilingual Research Journal, 23*, 113–134.

Moll, L. C., & Dworin, J. E. (1996). Biliteracy development in classrooms: Social dynamics and cultural possibilities. In D. Hicks (Ed.), *Child discourse and social learning* (pp. 221– 246). Cambridge, UK: Cambridge University Press.

Moschkovich, J. (2006). Using two languages when learning mathematics. *Educational Studies in Mathematics, 64*, 121–144.

Ramírez, D., Pasta, D., Yuen, S., & Ramey, D. (1991). *Final report. Longitudinal study of structured English immersion strategy, early-exit and late-exit transitional bilingual education programs for language-minority children*. San Mateo: CA: Aguirre International.

Reyes, I. (2004). Functions of code switching in schoolchildren's conversations. *Bilingual Research Journal, 28*(3), 77–98.

Slavin, R., & Cheung, A. (2003). *Effective reading programs for English language learners: A best-evidence synthesis.* Washington, DC: Center for Research on the Education of Students Placed at Risk (CRESPAR).

Sparrow, W., Butvilofsky, S., & Escamilla, K. (2012). The evolution of biliterate writing through simultaneous bilingual literacy instruction. In E. Bauer & M. Gort (Eds.), *Early biliteracy development: Exploring young learners' use of their linguistic resource* (pp. 157–181). New York, NY: Routledge.

Thomas, W., & Collier, V. (1997). *School effectiveness for language minority students.* Washington, DC: National Clearinghouse for Bilingual Education.

Tse, L. (1996). Language brokering in linguistic minority communities: The case of Chinese- and Vietnamese-American Students. *Bilingual Research Journal, 20*, 485–498.

Valdés, G., & Figueroa, R. A. (1994). *Bilingualism and testing: A special case of bias.* Norwood, NJ: Ablex.

Wei, L. (2000). Dimensions of bilingualism. In. L. Wei (Ed.), *The bilingualism reader* (pp. 3–25). New York, NY: Routledge.

Zehler, A., Fleischman, H., Hopstock, P., Stephenson, T., Pendzick, M., & Sapru, S. (2003). *Descriptive study of services to LEP students and LEP students with disabilities: Vol. 1. Research Report.* Retrieved from http://onlineresources.wnylc.net/pb/orcdocs/LARC_Resources/LEPTopics/ED/DescriptiveStudyofServicestoLEPStudentsandLEPStudentswithDisabilities.pdf

CHAPTER 8

Scaffolding Discussions to Develop Comprehension and Students' Voices

Josephine Arce
Elizabeth Padilla Detwiler

There was excitement in the air as 25 eighth graders walked into their homeroom to begin Eco Summit I Day. These students were presenting their project-based research papers on social and ecological issues affecting local and global environments. After 6 weeks of study, this final project and culminating event simulated a social science conference day, with the classroom rearranged into panel tables for the speakers and a lecture forum for their peer audience. There were five groups, each with five presenters/panelists addressing their positions on student-selected topics such as Healthy Styles, Clean Air, Clean Water, World Hunger, and Public Transportation. All the panelists assumed the role of academics and scientists and were addressed with the title of Doctor along with their surname. In addition to students presenting as panelists, they comprised an audience that actively listened, took notes to use for follow-up activities, and responded to questions at the end of each session.

Students also designed action plans to take place in their school and surrounding community. This cumulative and transformative educational process ended with students conducting service learning activities to put their newly gained knowledge into practice: teaching kindergartners how to make healthy snacks, planting trees with the League of Urban Foresters, packing lunches for the neighborhood homeless for 3 weeks, encouraging students and their families to use public transportation, and bicycling or walking to school.

In this chapter we attempt to describe the learning environment the teacher developed for these eighth graders and how project-based instruction supported in-depth learning experiences while contributing to the development of students' social and political consciousness. We also describe how key literacy strategies and discussions were constructed and scaffolded (Wood, Bruner, & Ross, 1976) to support English language learners' and native speakers' development of critical content knowledge and contributed to students' overall increase in comprehension.

CRITICAL PEDAGOGY AND SOCIOCOGNITIVE THEORY

Two central theories are used to describe how teachers can engage students in meaningful learning experiences that accelerate their academic skills while contributing to the development of social consciousness. First, critical pedagogy provides a framework for educators to understand the role that schools play in reproducing social and economic inequities. In fact, schools are generally places to reproduce the ideologies of those in power (Balderrama & Díaz-Rico, 2006; Darder, 1991; Darder, Baltodano, & Torres, 2009; Freire, 1970/2004; McLaren, 2003). Second, sociocognitive theory is the framework that supports our work as it relates to literacy supports for learning (Langer, 1986, 2001; Rosenblatt, 2004).

Critical Pedagogy: Political Clarity Guiding Teaching Decisions

McLaren (2003) states that schooling is a form of cultural politics in that it represents an introduction to, preparation for, and legitimizing of particular forms of social life. It perpetuates forms of knowledge that support specific views of the past, present, and future based on relations of power, and social practices that reflect capitalism (pp. 186–187). Yet schools can also work toward uniting knowledge and power to critique social relations and question inequities with the goal of creating social justice (Darder, 1991; Giroux, 1981, 1983; McLaren, 2003). Giroux (1983) proposes that although schools have a major role as transmitters for capitalist interests, they also serve as locations for opposition to the economic and political interests of dominant groups. Classrooms represent microcommunities that consist of people constructing meaning, challenging truths, negotiating, and producing on a daily basis. Teachers and students are not passive recipients accepting the dominant views or structures that maintain social inequities. He offers a theory of resistance within critical pedagogy, which explains how educators and students do resist dominant forms of oppression

(Giroux, 1981). These are not random acts of individuals but practices that intend to explore, uncover, and lead toward emancipation.

Many concepts in critical pedagogy incorporate Freire's (1970/2004) theoretical framework that examines the relationship between individuals and the world. People are more than spectators in the world; they live as active beings that name their world by re-creating new social, economic, and political relationships. An understanding of critical theory and pedagogy supports teachers envisioning possibilities that are democratic and emancipatory for the classroom community.

Teachers with political clarity, as identified by Bartolomé and Balderrama (2001), have a deep awareness of sociopolitical and economic realities that shape our lives and have the capacity to transform our lives. The classroom conditions for students to read beyond the printed word, to obtain deeper meaning of literature, and to analyze expository texts are deeply tied to a teacher's view of literacy. Often teachers are the key persons who provide learning experiences that help students read the world. Teachers with critical consciousness examine their beliefs about teaching and the instructional approaches they select to support English language learners (ELLs). Their pedagogy is closely tied to their view of power relations at a societal level. These teachers question injustices and inequities by seeking ways to redress and ultimately contribute to transforming the schooling of marginalized students. They understand that equity means preparing students with strong academic capacities that will facilitate their ability to navigate in multiple environments. The ability to read to learn and write to communicate with a purpose at proficient levels is a social justice issue (Almasi & Garas-York, 2009).

Supporting students to develop higher levels of comprehension of both narrative and expository texts stems from the opportunities teachers create in the classroom. How a teacher defines literacy development is central to the conditions that are provided for students' interactions with quality texts. Yet higher level transactions with texts do not come simply from selecting well-written texts or teaching effective strategies and methods that improve comprehension; it is much more complex. We argue that a teacher who strives to provide powerful academic learning opportunities integrated with social justice themes holds a political perspective that is grounded in critical pedagogy. The ability for these students to engage in dialogues concerning social conditions helps them construct deeper meanings that *transcend* the experience of reading and writing. In conjunction with effective literacy strategies, the teacher plays a major role in guiding students to develop their voices and their sense of social justice (Almasi & Garas-York, 2009).

Sociocognitive Theory: Supporting Literacy Practices

Rosenblatt's *The Reader, The Text, The Poem* (1978) presented the author's seminal theoretical framework of transactional theory that guides us to understand how readers construct meaning as they interact with text. Rosenblatt (2004) claims that every reading act is an event, or a transaction, involving a particular reader and a particular text. In other words, meaning cannot be imposed on the reader, but results from the complex, nonlinear, recursive, and self-correcting transaction between the reader and the printed page. She views the reading process as one where the reader adopts, consciously and unconsciously, a stance that brings certain aspects of the text into the center of attention and pushes others into the fringe of consciousness. Therefore, the transaction is between the reader and the text as the reader transforms the symbols on the page into a more meaningful piece, such as a passage or a poem (Rosenblatt, 1978). Readers bring their own experiences and background knowledge to the reading, changing their stance with the text. It is the type of meaning that each reader creates that makes each response different. Thus this meaning is the essence of comprehension. Teaching students to engage in texts, learn how to make connections to the text, and simultaneously connect one text to other texts, to themselves, and to their worldview contributes to higher levels of comprehension (Rosenblatt, 2004).

A reader's need to obtain meaning is the driving force behind language performance and reading growth. Block and Pressley (2007) and Blanton, Wood, and Taylor (2010) state that in order for readers to read more complex text they need the social interaction among their teachers and peers to understand how reading works and to successfully construct meaning and comprehension. They propose that comprehension depends on more than simply the reader's transaction with text.

Langer (1987) urges educators and researchers of literacy to take a sociocognitive view of language and literacy learning. This view recognizes that the contexts within which literacy is used and learned lead to particular ways of thinking and that culture (including the culture of the classroom), language, and cognition are inextricably intertwined. Literacy moves beyond the act of reading and writing, but is fundamentally based on the learners' interaction with their world and their ability to use their literacy skills to think, revise, and rethink as they transact with their world. It is a way of thinking, not simply reading and writing (Langer, 1987; Langer & Applebee, 1986).

Students can advance beyond their responses to text by having opportunities to act upon their ideas. As adolescents are developing a sense of self in relation to the world, they need ample support to express and explore avenues that can lead to social changes. Langer (2001) states that students typically do much better when instruction builds on previous knowledge and current ideas and experiences, permits students to voice their understandings and refine them through substantive discussion with others, and explicitly provides the new knowledge and strategies that students need to participate successfully in the continuing discussion.

Although there is extensive research about student response to texts (Almasi & Garas-York, 2009; Brabham & Villaume, 2000; Goldman & Rakeshaw, 2000; Langer, 1982, 1986, 2000; McLaughlin & DeVoogd, 2004; Pressley, 2000; Rosenblatt, 1978, 2004; Roser & Keehn, 2002), it offers limited descriptions of what those interactions actually look like in a classroom of upper elementary or middle school students. Even fewer models are presented in classrooms where the majority of the students are ELLs or those who come from culturally and linguistically minority backgrounds, and in many cases from lower socioeconomic backgrounds.

THE STUDY

This study looks at the life of an eighth-grade classroom explored through the eyes of the classroom teacher and a university researcher as they sought to examine the ways in which opportunities were provided to ELLs that allowed them to make meaning of content area texts and succeed in school. It focuses on how the classroom teacher provided language and content scaffolds (Wood et al., 1976) to make content comprehensible to the students. We ask two questions: How does a teacher design instruction within a social studies curriculum for ELLs while addressing and integrating literacy structures to facilitate comprehension? How does one teacher use metacognitive and cognitive strategies to teach content area literacy to ELLs?

This chapter presents the classroom structure that one of the authors, Elizabeth, created for her eighth-grade students guided by teaching decisions related to critical pedagogy, political clarity and sociocognitive theory, and view of language and literacy learning. The majority of students were ELLs at early and intermediate levels of proficiency who spoke English well at a social communicative level, but struggled with academic literacy.

The Students

The 25 students we highlight in this study were all living in a sorthern California urban center and attended a small Catholic school, San Miguel-Nativity (a pseudonym). The school is in the heart of a neighborhood where there are many marginalized groups mixed with low-income families of color. However, most of the students came from diverse, working-class communities where the majority of residents are people of color. In 2006 the student population in the school was 85% Latino, 10% Southeast Asian, and 5% African American. Many students were performing below grade level and were considered to be struggling with literacy. The school served Grades 4 through 8 with a student-teacher ratio of 12:1, but during integrated courses such as reading and language arts combined with social studies there could be as many as 20 students. Accepting students at the upper elementary and middle school levels was intentional, with the focus to prepare them for high school.

All 25 eighth-grade students were on full scholarships and the majority were ELLs. Their parents were immigrants and English was not the home language, but many of the students were born in the United States. Instruction focused on academic skills and cognitively demanding strategies through reading and language arts and content subjects, while also developing social awareness. The teachers met regularly to plan and share common academic and social goals. All the teachers used a comprehensive portfolio system, teacher annotated observations, grade-level standards, adopted texts, supplemental resources, and a standard individual student education plan. Social justice was also a primary mission of the school, allowing teachers more autonomy and flexibility to explore age-appropriate themes that contributed to students' understanding and practices of equity. Throughout the year students were immersed in appropriate grade-level literacy structures such as literature circles, critical discussions, and writing responses to literature reflecting social justice issues.

The Teacher

Elizabeth, a classroom teacher of this group of middle school students and one of the authors of this chapter, placed a strong emphasis on building community at the beginning of the school year. Her goal stemmed from the pedagogical principle that a sense of belonging allows students to envision how microcommunities can function effectively. In her classroom, along with building a respectful and caring community, students gradually learn to take more responsibility for their learning, as well as to set goals for their own futures.

Initially, Elizabeth taught most of the students during their first summer session before entering sixth grade and then became their sixth-grade teacher. She also followed the students to seventh grade as their reading and language arts instructor. Because the middle school teachers felt a particular urgency to prepare the eighth-grade students for a smooth transition to high school, they designed core instructional sections, such as in humanities, similar to high school structures. Therefore, as this group of students entered eighth grade, Elizabeth became their core humanities teacher combining reading and language arts with social studies.

In this particular classroom situation, due to the small class size and most students knowing each other, Elizabeth was able to create a community of trust between students and herself. Because Elizabeth had taught most of the same students in sixth and seventh grades, she created conditions for students' familiarity with many instructional strategies she used including journal writing, peer discussions, guided learning experiences, and project-based learning. Although most students traveled with Elizabeth to each grade level, several enrolled at different intervals and newer students had to learn how to apply learning strategies and social norms. The opportunity to follow former students allowed for maximum conditions to facilitate project-based learning; however, it is important to state that the efforts to build community were not weakened, but continued as a central element in Elizabeth's planning.

SCAFFOLDING STRATEGIES FOR
TEACHING CONTENT AREA LITERACY

Elizabeth was expected to cover the social studies curriculum in her classroom, yet most of the students needed improvement in their literacy development. As one of her primary goals was to develop critical and high-literacy thinkers, she made a conscious decision to apply a twin-text approach that integrated historical fiction with expository texts to support students' comprehension (Graesser, McNamara, & Louwerse, 2003; Kucan, Lapp, Flood, & Fisher, 2007). Elizabeth believed that a twin-text instructional approach would motivate students to make stronger personal connections with the characters and events in the historical and biographic texts. These learning opportunities could potentially expand their connections to broader social issues. Elizabeth explicitly addressed literacy strategies during the social studies block to facilitate their comprehension of content (Neufield, 2005). Students were expected to apply their literacy knowledge in a realistic setting that helped solidify the concept that literacy is not an isolated event, but rather the underlying framework for content area study and real-life applications. Thus Elizabeth explicitly taught literacy skills and metacognitive strategies to improve their approach to learning.

Engaging Students

In one unit on ecological issues, "Man vs. Nature" and "Man and Nature" were guiding themes used to invite students to think deeply and discuss the distinctions between the two perspectives and how these different views affect policies and political decisions. Choosing broad themes allowed students to read and select different material and also to explore specific topics of interest to them. Before beginning the project, Elizabeth used the *backward planning* approach where teachers consider three critical points: (1) student learning outcomes, (2) determining acceptable evidence or performance for the learning outcomes, and (3) planning activities based on the intended outcomes and the evidence and performance criteria for the entire unit (Kucan et al., 2007, p. 301). Because Elizabeth knew her students well, she was able to select literacy strategies that supported their learning outcomes. She searched for resources that provided context and content; reviewed the eighth-grade language arts and social studies standards; and selected specific historical fiction, short stories, poetry, and expository texts. Using backward planning allows the teacher to analyze, revise, and refine decisions in order to maximize what students can learn and demonstrate evidence of the learning. Central to this instructional plan and approach is the expectation that students will use their prior skills and knowledge by activating and drawing upon their background knowledge in relation to story content to support comprehension and vocabulary retention (Ulanoff & Pucci, 1999). As Langer (2001) suggests, Elizabeth also supported student learning by scaffolding lessons and employed newly introduced skills and knowledge within activities.

Multiple Texts

Elizabeth created an Eco Reader consisting of various texts aligned to the eighth-grade social studies curriculum and standards related to the two central themes previously mentioned. Her purpose for selecting the texts was to help students develop deeper understanding of the themes and to learn how to use genres in flexible ways. Thus, by giving students access to varied material that made learning easier as well as opportunities for reviewing and analyzing specific genre features, students became more skillful and strategic in selecting a genre to meet their research aim. Elizabeth also provided resources and opportunities for students to apply known and new skills and concepts into integrated events on a daily basis.

Elizabeth used book talks to motivate students about the themes or subtopics by introducing the author, stating his or her contributions to ecological issues, and discussing text features. She also selected one or two short stories or poems per week to read aloud to the class. Elizabeth believed it was critical to use read-alouds, particularly with her ELL students because they provide opportunities to hear the articulation of English words, phrases, and use of punctuation and to learn new word meanings (Hickman, Pollard-Durodola, & Vaughn, 2004). Struggling readers also benefit from read-alouds by listening to fluent reading and hearing the reader's aesthetic stance while appreciating the beauty of language, which can help the listener make connections with the story and the author. More important, throughout the unit, the read-alouds contributed to building community for all of the learners (including Elizabeth) by creating an aesthetic experience stimulated by the texts through whole-class discussions, allowing students to make comments and respond to open-ended questions. Thus Elizabeth went beyond just reading books and used these focused discussions after the read-alouds to help students work collaboratively and comprehend the stories (Cunningham & Allington, 2011; Ulanoff & Pucci, 1999). These discussions also served as informal assessments for their teacher (Lloyd, 2004).

Minilessons

Throughout her teaching, Elizabeth delivered minilessons on metacognitive strategies including think-alouds (Vacca, Vacca, & Mraz, 2010), self-monitoring (Hiebert, Skalitzky, & Tesnar, 1998), self-correcting, and cognitive strategies such as reciprocal teaching (Brown & Palincsar, 1986), questioning the author (Beck & McKeown, 2006), note taking, graphic organizers (Hall & Strangman, 2002), and sum-marizing orally and in writing (see Table 8.1). Students were also taught content vocabulary and academic language (e.g., semantic, syntax, and functional language use). Although most of the students returned and improved in their reading and writing every academic year, Elizabeth revisited and modeled these strategies because some students continued to need support as they encountered more com-plex academic tasks.

For example, during reciprocal reading practice, students made adaptations by using Post-it notes and writing predictions, questions for clarification, or points of confusion in their journals. For struggling ELLs, Elizabeth extended this adaptation to scaffold their learning, recognizing that ELLs need additional anchors and multiple opportu-nities to apply new strategies and that it takes time for them to fully internalize and comprehend the text. She also believed that automa-ticity requires extensive opportunities to analyze how to use strategies and apply them throughout various learning situations.

Students also had multiple ways to employ strategies and to self-evaluate, including using checklists. Thus Elizabeth would circulate and ask individuals to identify a strategy and their rationale for using it. She wanted to observe and evaluate if frequent practice and ap-plication of these strategies in fact helped them understand the texts more efficiently and with deeper analysis. Elizabeth also implemented daily informal assessments, which included observations, reviewing the quality of their assigned tasks, and noting if the assignments were completed in an appropriate time frame.

Structures for Reading Texts

Students were allowed to sit wherever they wanted during inde-pendent reading, with or without a partner, or in small groups. During students' reading in various group configurations Elizabeth describes her role:

> I would circulate around the room, sitting in with pairs or individuals to listen, scaffold, or briefly model fluent reading and think-alouds. In these situations I sometimes asked students to explain how they problem-solved.

Struggling ELLs were encouraged to take risks and use strate-gies such as self-monitoring and self-correcting. During minilessons, explicit explanations reinforced how using these strategies helped

TABLE 8.1. Metacognitive and Cognitive Strategies

Strategy	Description/Example
Think-alouds[1]	A strategy used to model the thought processes that take place when reading challenging material. The teacher verbalizes his or her thoughts while reading orally with the goal of having students understand comprehension strategies as the teacher models how to think things through as students are reading. Think-aloud procedures include making predictions, creating mental pictures, using analogies, and monitoring comprehension.
Self-monitoring[2]	Self-monitoring comprehension can be done as part of a think-aloud protocol or as a stand-alone strategy. When students self-monitor they think about what they have read before moving on to a new portion of the text. This helps students to reflect on and comprehend the text.
Self-correcting	Self-correcting is a strategy that students use during reading. It can involve making and confirming predictions, finding embedded definitions in text, or connecting meaning of new words to prior knowledge.
Reciprocal teaching (RT)[3]	RT is a teacher-guided instructional activity that takes place in the form of a dialogue between teachers and students regarding different pieces of text. The dialogue uses four strategies that students are taught: summarizing, question generating, clarifying, and predicting. The teacher and students are active participants, taking turns performing the role of teacher in leading the dialogue.
Questioning the author (QTA)[4]	QTA is a technique in which students learn how to take on more difficult text during reading with the teacher constructing meaning based on asking a series of questions. Students read and discuss a piece of text, answering such questions as: What is the author trying to say? Why is the author telling you that? Does the author state it clearly? What would you say instead? Active meaning is emphasized.
Note-taking strategies	There are a variety of note-taking strategies that students can use, including dialectical journals, where they write down direct quotes from the texts and then react to those quotes; writing summaries of chunks of texts; and highlighting key concepts.
Graphic organizers[5]	Graphic organizers are visual and graphic displays that depict the relationships between facts, terms, and/or ideas within a learning task. Graphic organizers include knowledge maps, concept maps, story maps, cognitive organizers, advance organizers, and concept diagrams.

1. Vacca, Vacca, & Mraz, 2010. 2. Hiebert et. al., 1998. 3. Palincsar, 1986; Brown & Palincsar, 1986. 4. Beck & McKeown, 2006, p. 29. 5. Hall & Strangman, 2002, p. 1.

students reach the broader learning goals. Moreover, during lessons Elizabeth acted intentionally in ways that modeled for students how to use strategies, self-monitor, and apply new learning to their own activities. She also provided students with opportunities to practice using strategies during guided and independent practice activities after the minilessons.

Elizabeth modeled how to analyze and use high-level vocabulary and academic content vocabulary. The primary strategies students used to unfold challenging vocabulary included understanding how to use affixes and word patterns (Cunningham & Allington, 2011). Students learned content vocabulary through using cognates, word maps, and word jeopardy games with the entire class. Older struggling readers also needed support on how to apply strategies at the word level and how to apply metacognitive and cognitive strategies throughout the reading and writing processes to achieve successful comprehension (Block & Pressley, 2007).

Elizabeth believed that applying cognitive strategies to students' activities was critical. It was particularly important to observe how ELLs problem-solved semantic miscues in pairs or small groups. Although Elizabeth supported students extensively helping each other, one of the learning outcomes included students' learning how to apply strategies and gradually becoming independent problem solvers. For example, students were taught strategies such as (1) rereading a phrase or the whole sentence; (2) searching text features such as subheadings: (3) analyzing word patterns; (4) creating visual representations; and (5) thinking aloud to predict, check, and confirm (Goldman & Rakestraw, 2000; Massey & Heafner, 2004).

Students were also expected to improve their abilities on a daily basis, and although some did not master every strategy or skill, ultimately they were expected to make substantial gains at the end of the unit. In an effort to differentiate instructional plans, a teacher must make connections between skills, practice, and purpose so that all students have access to the content. Elizabeth understood how important these connections were to helping students understand how to do well and to think about their tasks (Langer, 2001). She also knew it was important to *integrate and still differentiate* the scaffolding in explicit teaching during individual and small-group encounters by providing a variety of language and content supports to allow students to meaningfully engage in content area learning and acquire the necessary language and academic skills necessary for independent learning. For adolescent readers, the texts became harder and more abstract and many students needed support to problem-solve while using comprehension processes at multiple levels throughout their reading and writing. While ELLs and struggling readers made significant gains, many continued to struggle with comprehension and higher level vocabulary. Since these learners had to work hard at literacy, teaching new or revisiting older problem-solving strategies was essential.

Writers' Journals

Early in the year Elizabeth modeled how to respond to open-ended questions on an overhead transparency and students critiqued the strengths of her samples. When she asked, "What else could I add to make this clearer to show how much I know?" the class contributed their suggestions, and she revised and compared drafts. As students began their own writing, she wanted them to put their ideas and responses on paper without too much concern about spelling and punctuation. This free-flowing writing was particularly helpful for ELLs as they gradually improved on their spelling, grammar, and punctuation.

In order for students to understand the form, flow, and purpose of the writer's journal, Elizabeth guided students through the process, starting with connections to their previous writing experiences. As a class, they decided on the key features to include or exclude in a writer's notebook. This discussion was recorded on a T-chart with the headings "a writer's notebook looks/sounds like" written on one side and "a writer's notebook doesn't look/sound like" on the other side and posted in the front of the room. Using this approach, Elizabeth instructed in ways to teach writing conventions, such as spelling and grammar, as *separate instruction* not taught in isolation but within the *meaningful* activities of a unit (Langer, 2001). Thus she provided students with opportunities for learning practical conventions, allowing students' success in the actual activities.

Students used a multipurpose journal (Langer & Applebee, 1986) as a place to make connections, construct meaningful responses, and chronicle the relationship between the literature and their projects. The journals served many different purposes: (1) keeping notes on narrative and expository elements; (2) drawing illustrations; (3) using graphic organizers; (4) describing episodes; (5) problem posing; (6) stating characters and author's purposes; (7) stating readers' concerns, confusions, questions and writing clarifications; and (8) responding to films or Internet reports. These notes helped students synthesize information for writing essays and reports and as a preparation for group discussions.

Learning by Scaffolding and Behavior Expectations

Central to the classroom community were *peer scaffolding* and *guided discussions*—particularly for ELLs—to encourage higher level thinking and more elaborate responses related to vocabulary (Au, 1993). By giving students choices on the composition of their groups, Elizabeth allowed them to share information, check their predictions, identify information, and clarify, revise, and gather new information.

In addition, Elizabeth provided ways to lessen student dependency on teacher feedback by teaching them how to self-check, get peer feedback, and listen to group feedback. Elizabeth believed that self-evaluation helped students create ownership and contributed to self-efficacy (Bandura, 1997). In addition, students seemed better prepared to present their ideas when they had time to talk about them and allow for positive critical feedback from other student group members.

Early in the year Elizabeth paired less proficient ELLs with stronger readers or native speakers in multiple ways in order to support and maximize the learning opportunities for everyone. For example, high-progress students needed opportunities to work with equally strong peers but also needed to practice how to support less proficient peers. While these students were not expected to replace the teacher, they offered support and collaborated with each other. However, students who needed more academic support initially met daily with Elizabeth and later in the year became much more independent.

The classroom's academic and behavior expectations were clearly stated and written on the board. These expectations included students practicing reading strategies as they read, completing assignments that led to research, journal writing, gathering notes, writing report drafts, and completing final oral and written reports. Elizabeth observed that when students know the academic and behavioral expectations, they appear to be more focused, are able to evaluate their progress and complete assignments, know how to apply skills or strategies, and utilize peer feedback. Elizabeth's teaching philosophy included the premise that students respond well to responsibility and to having choices in their environments (Echevarria & Graves, 2003). Thus students were empowered by these choices to engage in research and were able to see a purpose to their selected projects. By creating a learning environment where the content applied to the students' interests, they were critically engaged and developed a sense of agency.

Impact of Discussions on Comprehension

From a sociocultural perspective, learning occurs when the learner can enter into dialogue with others, sharing his or her ideas, culture, language styles, and knowledge (Almasi & Garas-York, 2009; Langer, 1986; Langer & Applebee, 1986). Moreover, Almasi and Garas-York (2009) argue that the nature of dialogue enables learners to observe and interact with more knowledgeable others as they engage in cognitive processes that are accessible independently. According to these scholars, learning occurs incidentally, allowing the learners to internalize higher cognitive functions, such as interpreting literature or monitoring one's comprehension (p. 472). In this classroom, students were at the center of their group discussions. Their teacher observed, modeled, and facilitated when necessary and requested that students provide their own questions. In small groups of three to five, students created their own conversations and questions about their readings. Elizabeth believed that using this approach allows students to be able to support each other in their level of discussions, while using critical thinking skills through their own questioning and responses (Brabham & Villaume, 2000). This process takes time to develop and some students were more adept at leading discussion groups and possessing strong literacy skills, while others struggled initially.

However, as peers raise opinions, predictions, and higher level questions, there is a danger that some students could use their verbal or personal skills as a form of power. Yet Moller's (2004) research on struggling readers' response to text within small discussion groups informs us that power struggles can be diffused when teachers create a classroom culture of respect, acceptance, and intolerance for taunting. Moller describes a truly interactive learning community as built not on one group being the *children-who-know* and another being the *children-who-are-helped-to-know*, but rather built on *honest respect* for self and others. Thus students honor the notion that each person is a full member who has something valuable to offer. Elizabeth understood that the success of small groups depended on how much students believed in collaboration and respect toward one another and that much of the success resulted from the community building she had developed with the class. For example, as some of the struggling readers initially contributed more by retelling of the texts, as their peers raised opinions, predictions, and higher level questions, they began to provide critical questions. Every member of a group brought their intellectual and social capital to contribute to the group's learning outcomes, whether it was their motivation, literacy strengths, communication skills, or their inquisitive nature.

CONCLUSION

We have provided a window into Elizabeth's middle school classroom that reflects the linguistic and cultural diversity found in most urban classrooms. However, it is not a typical classroom, because Elizabeth promoted critical and strategic learning opportunities for all her students, including ELLs and students struggling with literacy. She provided explicit teaching and various strategies, extensive student collaboration, student choice, and a variety of texts (genres, films, realia, newspapers, and the Internet) to support student academic and social development. Her commitment, political clarity, and sense of social justice were central to the success of the classroom community. We invited readers into this eighth-grade classroom with the hope of inspiring teachers to take risks, reflect upon their teaching philosophy, and select instructional approaches that impact students' opportunities to advance academically, while simultaneously developing their social consciousness through meaningful project-based learning.

REFERENCES

Almasi, J. F., & Garas-York, K. (2009). Comprehension and discussion of text. In S. E. Israel & G. G. Duffy (Eds.), *Handbook of research on reading comprehension* (pp. 470–493). New York, NY: Routledge.

Au, K. H. (1993). *Literacy instruction in multicultural settings.* New York, NY: Harcourt Brace.

Balderrama, M. V., & Díaz-Rico, L. T. (2006). *Teaching performance expectation for educating English learners.* New York, NY: Pearson.

Bandura, A. (1997). *Self-efficacy: The exercise of control.* New York, NY: W. H. Freeman.

Bartolomé, L. I., & Balderrama, M. (2001). The need for educators with political and ideological clarity: Providing our children with "the best." In M. Reyes & J. Halcón (Eds.), *The best for our children: Latina/Latino views on literacy* (pp. 48–64). New York, NY: Teachers College Press.

Beck, I. L., & McKeown, M. G. (2006). *Improving comprehension with questioning the author: A fresh and expanded view of a powerful approach.* New York, NY: Scholastic.

Blanton, W. E., Wood, K. D., & Taylor, D. B. (2010). Rethinking middle school reading instruction: A basic activity. In M. Cappello & B. Moss (Eds.), *Contemporary readings in literacy education*. Thousand Oaks, CA: Sage.

Block, C. C., & Pressley, M. (2007). Best practices in teaching comprehension. In L. B. Gambrell, L. M. Morrow, & M. Pressley (Eds.), *Best practices in literacy instruction* (3rd ed., pp. 220–242). New York, NY: Guilford Press.

Brabham, E. G., & Villaume, S. K. (2000). Continuing conversations about literature circles. *The Reading Teacher, 54*(3), 278–280.

Brown, A. L., & Palinscar, A. (1986). *Reciprocal teaching of comprehension strategies: A natural history of one program for enhancing learning* (Technical Report No. 334). Champaign: University of Illinois, Center for the Study of Reading.

Cunningham, P., & Allington, R. L. (2011). *Classrooms that work: They can all read and write*. Boston, MA: Pearson.

Darder, A. (1991). *Culture and power in the classroom: A critical foundation for bilingual education*. Westport, CT: Bergin & Garvey.

Darder, A., Baltodano, M. P., & Torres, R. D. (Eds.). (2009). *The critical pedagogy reader* (2nd ed). New York, NY: Routledge.

Echevarria, J., & Graves, A. (2003). *Sheltered content instruction: Teaching English language learners with diverse abilities* (2nd ed.). Boston, MA: Allyn & Bacon.

Freire, P. (2004). *Pedagogy of the oppressed* (30th. ed., Myra Bergman Ramos, Trans.). New York, NY: Continuum. (Original work published 1970)

Giroux, H. A. (1981). *Ideology, culture, and the process of schooling*. Philadelphia, PA: Temple University Press.

Giroux, H. A. (1983). *Theory and resistance in education: A pedagogy for the opposition*. New York: Bergin & Garvey.

Goldman, S. R., & Rakestraw, J. A., Jr. (2000). Structural aspects of constructing meaning from text. In M. Kamil, P. B. Mosenthal, P. D. Pearson, & R. Barr (Eds.), *The handbook of reading research: Vol. 3* (pp. 311–335). Mahwah, NJ: Erlbaum.

Graesser, A. C., McNamara D., &. Louwerse, M. M. (2003). What do readers need to learn in order to process coherence relations in narrative and expository text? In A. P. Sweet & C. E. Snow (Eds.), *Rethinking reading comprehension* (pp. 82–98). New York, NY: Guilford Press.

Hall, T., & Strangman, S. (2002). *Graphic organizers*. Wakefield, MA: National Center on Accessing the General Curriculum. Retrieved from http://aim.cast.org/sites/aim.cast.org/files/NCACgo.pdf

Hickman, P., Pollard-Durodola, S., & Vaughn, S. (2004). Storybook reading: Improving vocabulary and comprehension for English-language learners. *The Reading Teacher, 57*(8), 720–730.

Hiebert, E. H., Skalitzky, K., & Tesnar, K. A. (1998). *Every child a reader*. Ann Arbor, MI: Center for the Improvement of Early Reading Achievement.

Kucan, L., Lapp, D., Flood, J., & Fisher, D. (2007). Instructional resources in the classroom: Deepening understanding through interactions with multiple texts and multiple media. In L. B. Gambrell, L. M. Morrow, & M. Pressley (Eds.), *Best practices in literacy instruction* (pp. 285–312). New York, NY: Guilford Press.

Langer, J. A. (1982). Facilitating text processing: The elaboration of prior knowledge. In J. A. Langer & M. Smith-Burke (Eds.), *Reader meets author/ bridging the gap: A psycholinguistic and sociolinguistic perspective.* Newark, DE: International Reading Association.

Langer, J. A. (1987). *A sociocognitive perspective on literacy.* In J. A. Langer (Ed.), *Language, literacy, and culture: Issues of society and schooling* (pp. 1–20). Norwood, NJ: Ablex.

Langer, J. A. (2000). Literary understanding and literature instruction (Research Report Series 2.11). Albany: State University of New York, National Research Center on English Learning and Achievement. Retrieved from http://www.albany.edu/cela/reports/langer/langerliteraryund.pdf

Langer, J. A. (2001). Beating the odds: Teaching middle and high school students to read and write well. *American Educational Research Journal, 38,* 837–880.

Langer, J. A., & Applebee, A. N. (1986). Reading and writing instruction: Toward a theory of teaching and learning. *Review of Research in Education, 13,* 171–194.

Lloyd, S. L. (2004). Using comprehension strategies as a springboard for student talk. *Journal of Adolescent and Adult Literacy, 48*(2), 114–124.

Massey, D. D., & Heafner, T. L. (2004). Promoting reading comprehension in social studies. *Journal of Adolescent and Adult Literacy, 48*(1), 26–40.

McLaren, P. (2003). *Life in schools* (4th. ed.). Boston, MA: Allyn & Bacon.

McLaughlin, M., & DeVoogd, G. (2004). Critical literacy as comprehension: Expanding reader response. *Journal of Adolescent and Adult Literacy, 48*(1), 52–62.

Moller, K. J. (2004). Creating zones of possibility for struggling readers: A study of one fourth grader's shifting roles in literature discussions. *Journal of Literacy Research, 36*(4), 419–460. Retrieved from http://jlr.sagepub.com/content/36/4/419.full.pdf

Neufield, P. (2005). Comprehension instruction in content area classes. *The Reading Teacher, 59*(4), 302–312.

Palincsar, A. S. (1986). The role of dialogue in providing scaffolded instruction. *Educational Psychologist, 21*(1/2), 73–98.

Pressley, M. (2000). What should comprehension instruction be the instruction of? In M. Kamil, P. B. Mosenthal, P. D. Pearson, & R. Barr (Eds.), *The handbook of reading research, Vol. 3* (pp. 545–561). Mahwah, NJ: Erlbaum.

Rosenblatt, L. M. (1978). *The reader, the text, the poem.* Carbondale: Southern Illinois University Press.

Rosenblatt, L. M. (2004). The transactional theory of reading and writing. In R. B. Ruddell & N. J. Unrau (Eds.), *Theoretical models and processes of reading* (5th ed.). Newark, DE: International Reading Association.

Roser, N. L., & Keehn, S. (2002). Fostering thought, talk and inquiry: Linking literature and social studies. *The Reading Teacher, 55*(5), 416–427.

Ulanoff, S. H., & Pucci, S. L. (1999). Learning words from books: The effects of read-aloud on second language vocabulary acquisition. *Bilingual Research Journal, 23*(1&2), 400–422.

Vacca, R. T., Vacca, J. L., & Mraz, M. E. (2010). *Content area reading: Literacy and learning across the curriculum* (10th ed.). Boston, MA: Allyn & Bacon.

Wood, D. J., Bruner, J. S., & Ross, G. (1976). The role of tutoring in problem solving. *Journal of Child Psychology and Psychiatry, 17*(2), 89–100.

CHAPTER 9

The Story of César Chávez High School

One Small School's Struggle for Biliteracy

Sandra Liliana Pucci
Gregory J. Cramer

A growing body of literature suggests important benefits of smaller high schools in comparison to their traditional "comprehensive" counterparts (Darling-Hammond, Acess, & Wichterle Ort, 2003; Shear et al., 2008). Such benefits reside in both the affective and academic domains. Proponents of small schools have reported more personalized environments in which teachers know all students, more positive feelings about self and school exhibited by students, more parental choice and involvement, and other relevant climate issues (Conchas & Rodríguez, 2008).

The transformation of two low-performing comprehensive high schools into smaller schools by the Coalition Campus School Project in New York City produced startling improvements in several areas: attendance, reading and writing assessments, graduation rates, and college-going rates (Darling-Hammond et al., 2003; Iatarola, Schwartz, Stiefel, & Chellman, 2008). Other research shows more access to higher level academic offerings and more equitable achievement gains (Lee & Ready, 2007). Data from the high school dropout literature focusing on school structure indicate that the social and academic organization of a school can have a significant impact (Lee & Burkham, 2003). Smaller school size can serve to "constrain" the curriculum, limiting offerings to more challenging, academic material rather than lower level courses, which in turn leads to higher and more equitably distributed learning (Lee, Croninger, & Smith, 1997).

At the present moment there is little research examining how Latino students fare in these smaller schools. The school that is the center of the case study described in this chapter was founded on the principles of best practices for language minority students, such as primary language instruction and support, preteaching vocabulary, and context-embedded instruction (Cloud, Genesee, & Hamayan, 2009; García, 2005; Goldenberg & Coleman, 2010). This research has shown that utilizing and developing the native language enhances academic achievement and English proficiency. Bilingual education in this school district is defined as a K–12 developmental program.

STUDYING CÉSAR CHÁVEZ HIGH SCHOOL

The focal school for this chapter is César Chávez High School (CCHS, a pseudonym), a bilingual, university-preparatory high school in the urban Midwest. CCHS was founded by nine bilingual high school teachers, their students, a university professor, and a group of parents. Their coming together was a product of several years of joint effort in a large, comprehensive high school, and the desire for a more effective and equitable education for bilingual students. The previous institution had a population of 1,500 and a 50% graduation rate. The group of nine teachers felt that their efforts to foster student achievement were "diluted" by other personnel in the building, who clearly did not share their vision. They had previously worked with the university professor as part of a federal grant aimed at effecting important changes, but when the principal of the school retired, things began to unravel. The group decided to found a new school. The climate to participate in such an undertaking was favorable, given that the district had just received funding from the Bill and Melinda Gates Foundation to support the start-up of a group of small high schools.

CCHS is categorized as an "instrumentality charter" of the district; in other words, all teachers are union members and employees of that school district. The chartering document, which states the mission of the school, cites transformative pedagogy, integrated curriculum, constructivism, college preparation, and the development of bilingualism/biliteracy as the shared vision. There is also an explicit commitment to antiracist, antilinguicist, antisexist, and anticlassist pedagogy. CCHS opened its doors in September of 2004 and is currently in its seventh year of operation.

CCHS enrolls 250 students, 95% of whom are Latino, with the majority being of Mexican or Caribbean origin. The students are largely placed in grade-level groups according to English and Spanish proficiency levels; these are malleable groups of "English-dominant," "Spanish-dominant," and "transitional." A *constrained curriculum,* which posits one set of academic objectives for all students regardless of individual needs (Lee et al., 1997), is the norm at the school, with students at each grade level receiving the same courses, all academic in nature. Enrollment goes through the same process used by the district and there are no entrance requirements. The school has no administrator and runs as a *teachers' cooperative*—a structure in which administrative duties are distributed among teaching staff.

This chapter presents a descriptive study of CCHS. Data collection began during the second year of the school's operation and focuses on exploring and describing the efforts of "founding members" in their struggle against "playing host to the system" (Bowles & Gintis, 1976) through the establishment of a progressive, university-preparatory school serving an overwhelmingly Latino English-language-learning population.

The researchers—a university professor (Pucci), who is also one of the founding members of the school, and two teachers (Cramer and one other teacher) enrolled in graduate studies at the university—used mixed methods to study CCHS. Data collection included classroom observations, observations of teacher meetings, and focus-group interviews of a purposive sample of students across grade levels. Selected classrooms were observed twice weekly by one of the researchers. Ethnographic field notes and audio recordings were collected during observations and interviews (Emerson, Fretz, & Shaw, 1995), and student artifacts were also collected. This chapter reports on data collected during the school's first five years of operation, with the student focus groups taking place in Year 3. The researchers have served in multiple roles: nonparticipant observers in the classroom, participant observers at meetings, full participants at meetings, as well as classroom teachers who acted as complete participants in their own teaching contexts (Gold, 1958; Junker, 1960). Observational field notes, audiotapes, student artifacts, online parent surveys, publicly available institutional data, and focus group and interview data (of students and teachers) were also collected during this time.

The data were analyzed, categorized, compared, and contrasted using a methodology that seeks to "elicit meaning from the data" (LeCompte & Preissle, 1993, p. 235), rather than codify and compute it. Instead, categories and domains are constructed (Spradley, 1980). A domain analysis was used to sort the data into multiple categories, allowing a portrait to emerge that is reflective of the big picture of the systems and issues affecting operation.

SUCCESSES AND CHALLENGES: EMERGING THEMES

The purpose of this study was to examine and describe factors that support or hinder the success of CCHS and its students. Several major themes emerged from the analysis of data collected over the first five years: community, political engagement, academics and curriculum, intellectual freedom, school district bureaucracy, and teacher consciousness.

Community

The majority of students and teachers in the school feel a strong sense of community and belonging. Students report that "everyone knows each other, and nobody got problems with each other." Several students and teachers used the term "family-like" to describe the atmosphere at the school. One student said "people actually pay attention to you here." The students feel that the teachers are "different, cool with us," and that they can discuss anything with the teachers. However, others felt that certain teachers "try to control us, and they can't." It is interesting to note that despite the fact that many students used the term "family-like" to describe the atmosphere, there are still important teacher-student tensions and misunderstandings. Yet we find an overwhelming *social* buy-in on the part of students.

Despite different cliques, the general sentiment is one of great respect among students; this fact is borne out by the extremely low incidence of any type of violence or fighting between students, in contrast with most large high schools in the district. Most students live in the neighborhood. There are also many siblings and cousins at CCHS and some of the teachers and staff have enrolled their own children. The majority of teachers also feel that the quality of student-teacher relationships on the school level is remarkably close. Although they had experienced close relationships with students while working in previous settings, they commented that the size of the school also influenced their interactions. Some teachers reported significant mentoring relationships with students whom they had never had in class.

Clearly, the establishment of community is one of the successes of the school.

Political Engagement

Students and teachers from CCHS are very active in the larger political context of immigration rights. Participation in locally and nationally organized protest marches are regular events. Several of the teachers and the university professor continue to push for college opportunities for "undocumented" students, who constitute a considerable portion of the school's population. The state in which the school is located recently passed a provision enabling undocumented students to be assessed resident tuition. Previously, according to statute they were assessed as international students, regardless of their graduation from a high school clearly located within the boundaries of the state. However, some state campuses continue to require the students to "apply" for such a tuition waiver—it is not automatic. Thus the students must expose themselves as undocumented in order to apply for the in-state tuition remission, something that is obviously problematic.

Furthermore, present and past students continue to be active in protesting what they view as interference in their school by the district, due to low test scores and NCLB regulations. They have regularly attended school board and other district level meetings. In October 2011 there was a walk-out, during which many former students and community members joined the students and staff.

Academics and Curriculum

Both teachers and students report high expectations for the quality of work students are required to complete. In the first three years CCHS was able to maintain its commitment to 6 years of mathematics in 4 years of high school, offering a full array of courses taught by qualified, licensed teachers. Courses such as the Spanish for Native Speakers (SNS) offerings have proven useful to a significant number of students. In 2010, 13 students scored well enough on the Advanced Placement (AP) Spanish language examination to obtain the retroactive college credits. Similarly, the social studies/language arts connection with Latino history and Latino literature courses, which all freshmen receive, has remained consistent despite staff turnover. By the fifth year of operation the World History curriculum had been transformed from a typical chronological representation of "facts" into a thematic, critical examination of the sociopolitical forces that have shaped the world. Unfortunately, this has not been true in all content areas. Science, for example, has been plagued by the general shortage of bilingual science teachers, as well as significant teacher turnover.

The Advanced Placement Debate. During Year 3 some important questions were raised regarding AP courses. Some teachers felt that their content and manner of delivery were incompatible with the CCHS mission of a truly culturally relevant and engaging curriculum. This is of particular importance, since despite the students' social buy-in, there are still those who remain academically unengaged. This theme also arose during student focus groups, with several students describing their courses as being "boring," or "something my grandmother would like." Students know they are "advanced" but want content they can relate to, "stuff we are going through," rather than "things that happened even before Christ was born."

The AP debate came to a head during the third year of operation. A group of teachers acting independently began to program the junior class (for their second semester) into two groups, students who wanted to combine AP U.S. history with an advanced English course entitled American Authors, and others who preferred "regular" English Eleven and "regular" U.S. history. Subsequent intervention and discussion led to more students in the "advanced" classes, but the result was, in effect, a tracked junior class, which students interpreted as separating the "*más cerebritos*" (brainiest) from the others, and as they were being separated from their friends, their lament was both academic and social. This set off an ideological alarm for some staff, who maintained that tracking was clearly against the school's philosophy. A new teacher, who was eventually assigned the regular U.S. history course, raised issues of both equity and pedagogy, as in his opinion, the "mix of higher and lower" achievers would have been healthier, resulting in more learning and prosocial behavior. One group of teachers was especially dismayed at the tracking, as the 11th graders were products of the school, meaning that most had attended since the beginning of their high school careers, so there was no one else to blame for their "lack of preparation."

"Explain." Students were eager to discuss their classroom experiences and were clear about what they expected from teachers. In other words, they did not want to have books "thrown at them," but they wanted teachers to *"explain"* and to keep explaining until the students understood, to show them how, not just tell them. In their eyes, a good teacher was a person who didn't give up, who "stayed with the students" during the lesson, made sure they understood, and tried different ways of getting things across. In some instances, students complained about material being covered too quickly. One student recounted that she went to school one day asking about the previous day's work, and the attitude of the teacher was "like it is already tomorrow." Other students reported being loaded with homework they were unable to complete due to after-school obligations such as jobs, helping their parents at their workplace, or picking up and taking care of younger siblings and cousins. Compounding those realities was the issue that the students sometimes did not understand the material well enough to do the homework independently and were penalized if they do not complete it. As one student commented, *"No es que no queramos, es que no entendemos"* [It's not that we don't want to do it, it's that we don't understand].

A Print-Rich Environment. The original chartering document for CCHS included a heavy emphasis on biliteracy development. An important part of the school's mission is to develop academic registers in both English and Spanish, and enable students to express themselves powerfully and bilingually in multiple genres of written communication.

Space for the new school was carved out from an existing middle school with dwindling enrollment, and there was no library at the site. The teachers decided to use an available classroom to set up a literacy center, stocking it with a large quantity of high-interest books both in Spanish and English. However, this center did not effectively function until Year 3 of the CCHS operation, as the demands of start-up, as well as an underestimation of the library skills needed for such an undertaking, resulted in slow progress. By the end of Year 2 the teachers, as well as the university professor, decided to prioritize getting the center functioning. After further surveying the students, more high-interest materials were purchased and made accessible.

The school also has a daily sustained silent reading (SSR) program which began in Year 5; the literacy center is the source for most of these reading materials. While the SSR program is most likely responsible for the modest increases in reading scores on standardized tests, not all the students have bought into the activity. Inadequate buy-in and lack of modeling on the part of some teachers is at the heart of the problem. Despite a great deal of support and education on its implementation and value, several teachers have been resistant to submitting to its discipline.

Intellectual Freedom

During the first three years of operation there was a general air of professional fulfillment and satisfaction among the staff with regard to course offerings. Teachers were able to offer Latino history, Latino literature, Spanish for native speakers, an array of mathematics courses, art history, holistic literature-based ESL, different music courses, film analysis, psychology, and sociology. Obtaining a charter license through the state enabled teachers to teach outside their licensure. The ability to offer a culturally relevant, broad-reaching, "Latino-centric" curriculum has been one of the major successes of the school. Additionally, grants that were awarded for charter school operation, as well as a district-level Gates Foundation grant for "smaller high schools," enabled CCHS to purchase substantial amounts of nontextbook print materials and technology. Although some staff felt that special electives were sometimes based more on teachers' tastes and expertise rather than on student interests, overall morale around these issues was high.

During Years 4 and 5 the tide shifted. The state changed the ability of teachers to teach outside their areas with charter licenses. The "highly qualified teacher" clause of No Child Left Behind (NCLB), which prohibits teaching outside of one's licensed content areas, began to be enforced by the district. Thus the charter license, a tremendous boon for small high schools, was trumped by NCLB. The school was no longer able to draw upon the "unlicensed" talents of the teaching staff. Bilingual teachers could not teach ESL, professional but unlicensed musicians could not teach music, college athletes could not teach physical education (PE), and trained, passionate dancers could not teach dance. Presently, the school is severely limited in what electives it can offer. Furthermore, the district has been threatening to shut down schools that cannot offer PE or art; yet being a small school, CCHS simply does not have the resources to hire full-time art and PE teachers. For a short period, while there was still a middle school in the building, art and PE teachers were shared. However, due to declining enrollment the middle school was shut down, and the school has returned to the same staffing dilemma.

School District Bureaucracy

All of the founding-member teachers had worked for the same large urban school district for a number of years before starting their school. Nevertheless, the bureaucracy of the district continues to present unexpected challenges. There is considerable tension between the school's unique vision of autonomy, originality, and flexibility, and the district's structures requiring accountability and conformity. The school's smaller size, teachers' cooperative structure, and corresponding lack of layers of support staff found in larger, more traditional settings became a heavy burden on the lead teacher, as well as other individuals assuming leadership roles. In addition, many "central office" meetings at the district took teachers' time away from their students and teaching. Other challenges included managing the budget, meeting testing requirements, and various tasks that were unconnected to student learning.

School Improvement Plan. Additionally, the school has come under scrutiny for not meeting "adequate yearly progress" (AYP) according to NCLB guidelines in its test scores since inception. The majority of the students are English language learners (ELLs) who, by definition, are a "nonproficient" subgroup. Standardized tests are given in the tenth grade, and each year schools need to demonstrate AYP, regardless of whether the students understand the language of the test. The resulting classification as a "school in need of improvement" within a "district in need of improvement" has resulted in the invasion of what we characterize as an NCLB "middle management." Many consultants and school district personnel visited the school to deliver mandatory professional development, often on such elementary topics as "Bloom's taxonomy," a session in which pocket-reference flip charts were distributed. Instead of focusing on the specific needs of the teachers, students, and school, professional development sessions emphasized general topics geared to instruction in English, and most presenters had no expertise in bilingual education. Rather, the sessions consisted of a series of generic sessions that form part of the district's overall response to NCLB. Furthermore, in 2010 the district, acting under NCLB guidelines, mandated a "School Improvement Plan" (SIP), which has come to dominate all staff meetings. Whereas in the past the CCHS staff devoted common meeting times to developing integrated courses and schoolwide Socratic seminars based on engaging, culturally responsive literature, all staff meetings focused on figuring out how to get "local data" into the SIP. Thus the focus of such gatherings has shifted from working on larger issues or developing rich curricula for the school's unique population to putting data into the SIP. Although NCLB has posed challenges for many urban schools, the impact on CCHS has been particularly acute as it openly threatens the mission of the school and disproportionately penalizes ELLs.

Staffing. Although CCHS can interview and select their teachers, a shortage of high school bilingual personnel continues to plague the district. It is important to note that programs in this district are "developmental" rather than "transitional," so teachers must be fluent in Spanish. Years 1 and 2 were particularly difficult, with "long-term substitutes" assigned to the building by the district and philosophically incompatible with the school. At the end of Year 1, two of the founding members exited themselves from the school on "incompatibility transfers." In the middle of Year 2, a highly skilled science teacher decided to return to Puerto Rico. A new teacher, who had been chosen through the school's interview process, walked out after 3 weeks. Another new teacher spent the academic year afraid of his students and was not invited to return for Year 3. Pleas to the school district for qualified teachers were often answered by *"no hay"* ("there aren't any"). Years 3 and 4 started with the school in a slightly better position regarding staffing, with the hiring of a few new teachers, but the shortage of bilingual high school teachers remained, with no relief on the horizon.

Further, the "highly qualified teacher" clause of NCLB continues to stymie efforts to find truly qualified educators. For example, an excellent licensed teacher from Mexico who worked effectively with students for the Spanish for native speakers classes was unable to pass the PRAXIS I, a "preprofessional skills" examination, and was eventually replaced by a monolingual substitute.

Teacher Consciousness: Constructing *"El Hombre Nuevo"*

The CCHS founding teachers moved from a large comprehensive high school with multiple layers of personnel performing various tasks (i.e., administrators, counselors, clerical personnel, and so on). Forming a teachers' cooperative and opening a new school has been a continuous struggle to transform their ways of thinking about professional responsibilities, the students, and each other. This was seen in two forms: inequitable work burdens, particularly felt by the lead teachers, and "baggage" in the form of unproductive attitudes and beliefs, which have proved difficult to shed, gone unexamined, or in some cases, reified.

As previously mentioned, of particular concern was the push to track the eleventh graders by some teachers. Reasons given for separating the students included some having "low skills" or others "being capable but not willing" to do the work. Individual staff blamed the lack of skills on one or two particularly poor teachers who eventually left the school, while others saw this issue as representing a retreat from the original CCHS mission. In Year 3 a "junior meeting" was called, which resulted in previously detracked students deciding for the AP offerings and others "choosing the easier class." The staff came to loggerheads: Tracking is against the original mission of the school, but the teachers of these advanced courses did not see all students as being capable of succeeding in this curriculum and would not teach them. In Year 4 the staff decided to disband the offering of the AP U.S. history and American Authors combination in favor of a more engaging theme-based curriculum they agreed was more consistent with best practices for language minority students. However, there are still many important conversations that need to take place, some of which go straight to the heart of the AP system and the high school curriculum itself.

With the small numbers of students and close monitoring of their progress, the school is fostering a great percentage of students on track to graduate on time. In fact, as previously noted, the graduation and college-going rates are far above district averages. But there are bumps along the way. A critical incident at the end of Year 2, when four ninth graders who had not passed all their classes were "flunked," again sounded alarm bells. This was not a staff consensus decision; it was made by a teacher responsible for programming. Interestingly, in this case, the small size of the school worked against these students, who were programmed again as ninth graders, repeating the entire first semester ninth-grade curriculum, including classes they had actually passed. Those who had completed sufficient credits by January were "promoted" to the tenth grade. This situation caused much hurt and resentment on the part of these students, who eventually left the school—one never graduated.

Another ideological tension identified is the relationship between the teacher as individual and the school as a whole. There are a few teachers who do not make sufficient effort to implement collectively agreed-upon schoolwide initiatives, such as SSR, rules about school uniforms, tardiness, use of cell phones, "hall walking," and other issues. Nonimplementation of SSR was observed well into the second year of its inception, with some teachers using the SSR 45-minute time slot for homework, correcting papers, not monitoring student activity, and so on. A few individuals view their noncompliance with various policies as righteous acts of resistance. At times, an oppositional situation developed, in which some teachers are the "bad guys," or the "enforcers," and the "righteous resisters" are the "cool" teachers. There was also misunderstanding of a few teachers who seemingly did not understand what it meant to be part of a teachers' cooperative, or were not willing to work together as a collective.

WHAT HAVE WE LEARNED AT CÉSAR CHÁVEZ HIGH SCHOOL?

Despite these bumps, graduation rates in the first five years were well above the district average of 50%; CCHS rates hovered between 88% and 96%. Ten students graduated with full tuition scholarships to the state's flagship university as a result of their participation in a summer precollege program, as well as meeting admission requirements. Students are regular recipients of scholarship money from private sources. For example, in 2006 seven of the CCHS seniors received scholarships for a total of $178,000 to assist in their university studies. These available figures for college enrollment data are impressive. From the first graduating class of 47 (in 2005), 23 students immediately enrolled at either a 2- or 4-year college, a rate of 49%; the average college-going rate of subsequent classes is 43%.

Results from this study highlight the significant, if not unexpected, challenges in founding and sustaining a small bilingual high school. They point to several meaningful accomplishments, as well as critical work to be done.

In many ways the concept of a constrained curriculum (Lee & Burkam, 2003) has worked both in principle and practice. Being a small school with limited staff, it is almost impossible to change a student's schedule if conflict occurs. CCHS is quite different from a large comprehensive high school, where students can often be reprogrammed—sometimes on teacher whim—into a "lower level" class or a nonacademic elective. In the context of the school in this study, this constrained curriculum has the power to mitigate against tracking, embracing one academically oriented curriculum for all. Although some teachers were left unsatisfied by the outcome of the AP U.S. history decision, they were able to resolve the issue collectively, then found themselves embroiled in the curricular fall out from NCLB.

An examination of student transcripts shows that there is little or no variation of courses in the freshman and sophomore years. Yet even with the liberationist vision of the original chartering documents, adults sometimes find it hard to enact truly transformative stances toward students and each other. Some students report differential treatment in terms of access to information, flexibility regarding independent studies, attendance, grading, discipline, and "second chances." Institutional capital, although seemingly distributed on a communitarian basis, still has "competitive" leaks (Stanton-Salazar, 2001) with certain students or groups of students able to curry more favor than others. Staff agree that more face-to-face time where philosophical and ideological questions can be raised is needed, yet meeting times are inevitably consumed by the nuts-and-bolts work needed to simply keep the school floating. In addition, the demands of NCLB paperwork—most notably the School Improvement Plan—eat up time the staff could devote to critical issues. But CCHS is not the first to be faced with this challenge; it is a situation that has been previously discussed in small teacher-led schools (Meier, 2002). Yet, as Meier insightfully points out, there needs to be time to "safely" navigate critical issues, and this time has been severely lacking.

Our work at CCHS has led us to call for the rethinking of what defines a challenging, academically oriented curriculum. The notion of AP constituting a "gateway" to college success seems to be a relatively unchallenged concept by the majority of educators in the United States. Discussions of equal access to AP take center stage (Solórzano & Ornelas, 2002), rather than a critical analysis of the stifling, traditional AP curriculum itself, the financial interests of the College Board, or the underbelly of this system. The fact that passing AP examinations can lead to retroactive university credits at some—not all—institutions of higher learning certainly could be used as a justification, a so-called return on the investment. At CCHS we have seen some utility in the case of AP Spanish, but a deeper analysis of the system—who wins and who loses—is required. At this school, the leap between a Latino-centric freshman year and the culturally subtractive emphasis and narrow scope and sequence of AP courses in subsequent years created a disjointed curriculum, which sent mixed messages.

Teachers' ideologies and beliefs must also be explored and clarified. In Year 3, with the calming of the "start-up" waters, other issues were able to float to the surface. There are differing beliefs among teachers; some feel that the school is for everyone and that we should work with all students no matter what the challenge, and others maintain that if a student does not comply with the disciplinary and academic demands of the school, "it's time to look for another school." These ideologies are also manifested in individual teachers' perceptions that they care more than others or that they understand the students better, and falling into the trap of commiserating with students in their complaints against other teachers, justified or not. Yet others seem to want to be "friends" with their students.

While the need for caring educators (Valenzuela, 1999) is undeniable, caring must not be substituted for a political commitment to challenge students to acquire the type of skills and knowledge necessary to become critical, active citizens (or noncitizens, as the case may be with so many of our students). Thus the notions of caring and advocacy need to be interrogated. To do so, teachers must acknowledge the inevitable contradiction between individual and community. Both Bowles & Gintis (1976) and Freire (1970) are very clear on these concepts. In the case of schooling, this contradiction consists of teachers educating students in the interests of society, however those interests may be defined. Students, for their part, often seek to use their schooling for personal ends. Thus conflicts between students and teachers are inevitable because schools, even and perhaps especially schools that seek to educate students to become critical actors, are inherently constraining. Schools and teachers that deny this contradiction or wish it away forfeit their historic roles as institutions that mediate the passage of students from childhood to adulthood. Teachers must understand that this contradiction characterizes every school. It is independent of particular students and particular teachers, and stands above whatever warmth or personal regard that individual students and teachers have for each other (Bowles & Gintis, 1976).

Ernesto "Che" Guevara, in his essay "Socialism and Man in Cuba," (1989) discusses the difficulty of constructing a new society with individuals who were born and conditioned in the old. While our comparison to the Cuban revolution may seem hyperbolic, what the founding documents of the school show, is just that: An attempt to forge a new school society, a different, more equitable way of relating and being. But the transition is difficult. Guevara comments:

> I think the place to start is to recognize this quality of incompleteness. . . . The vestiges of the past are brought into the present in the individual consciousness, and a continual labor is necessary to eradicate them. . . . The new society in formation has to compete fiercely with the past. The past makes itself felt not only in the individual consciousness—in which the residue of an education systematically oriented toward isolating the individual still weighs heavily—but also through the very character of the transition period in which commodity relations still persist. So long as it exists its effects will make themselves felt in the organization of production and, consequently, in consciousness. (p. 5)

As this study shows, changing the size of a school alone cannot transform a system resistant to accommodating innovation, or an inequitable educational culture that has been unconsciously reproduced. Though each individual (teacher) is both "a unique being and a member of society" (p. 5), it is clear that more consciousness needs to be developed in order to obtain the collective rewards of liberationist schooling.

CONCLUSIONS

The national high school graduation rates of Latino and other students of color in the United States reveal an ongoing system of inequity. Although there seems to be controversy in the literature as to what constitutes a "dropout" (Fry, 2010), all agree that a substantial number of Latinos either drop out of a U.S. high school—37% according to Fry—or simply do not complete high school, 42% according to figures disseminated by the National Council of La Raza (http://www.nclr.org). Extensive commentary on this is beyond the scope of this paper, but one interesting point is Fry's distinction between ELL and English-proficient Latino dropouts. His figures assert that lack of English language ability is an important characteristic of Latino dropouts, almost 59% of whom do not speak English well (p. 9). One can only speculate as to the negative impact of the lack of quality bilingual programs for most secondary students. The dropout rate for Latinos in the Midwestern district where this school is located hovers at around 40%. There is a definite need to expand the research literature examining institutional factors and the utility of a constrained curriculum, as well as to identify the factors that lead to the positive affective and academic results of smaller, bilingual high schools.

Differential access to university preparatory courses has been repeatedly documented in the literature (Stanton-Salazar, 2001; Valenzuela, 1999). Although some, including Kozol (2005), insist that integration and/or busing students of color to more affluent, suburban high schools is the key to high school graduation, few have actually tried to construct, along with families, a school with culturally/linguistically relevant curriculum *for them*. This study examines one such school attempting to do so. If supporting and hindering factors can be identified through an examination of data, this research may provide substantial indications of how to more effectively fight educational inequity.

REFERENCES

Bowles, S., & Gintis, H. (1976). *Schooling in capitalist America.* New York, NY: Basic Books.

Cloud, N., Genesee, F., & Hamayan, E. (2009). *Literacy instruction for English language learners.* Portsmouth, NH: Heinemann.

Conchas, G., & Rodríguez, L. (2008). *Small schools and urban youth: Using the power of school culture to engage.* Thousand Oaks, CA: Corwin Press.

Darling-Hammond, L., Acess, J., & Wichterle Ort, S. (2003). Reinventing high school: Outcomes of the Coalition Campus School Project. *American Educational Research Journal, 39*(3), 639–673.

Emerson, R., Fretz, R., & Shaw, L. (1995). *Writing ethnographic fieldnotes.* Chicago, IL: University of Chicago Press.

Freire, P. (1970). *Pedagogy of the oppressed.* New York, NY: Seabury Press.

Fry, R. (2010). *Hispanics, high school drop outs and the GED.* Washington, DC: Pew Hispanic Center.

García, E. (2005). *Teaching and learning in two languages: Bilingualism and schooling in the United States.* New York, NY: Teachers College Press.

Gold, R. (1958). Roles in sociological field observation. *Social Forces, 36,* 217–223.

Goldenberg, C., & Coleman, R. (2010). *Promoting academic achievement among English learners. A guide to the research.* Thousand Oaks, CA: Corwin Press.

Guevara, E. (1989). *Socialism and man in Cuba.* New York, NY: Pathfinder Press.

Iatarola, P., Schwartz, A., Stiefel, L., & Chellman, C. (2008). Small schools, large districts: Small school reform and New York City's students. *Teachers College Record, 110*(9), 1837–1878.

Junker, B. (1960). *Field work.* Chicago, IL: University of Chicago Press.

Kozol, J. (2005). *Shame of the nation: The restoration of apartheid schooling in America.* New York, NY: Crown.

LeCompte, M., & Preissle, J. (1993). *Ethnography and qualitative design in educational research.* San Diego, CA: Academic Press.

Lee, V., & Burkam, D. (2003). Dropping out of high school: The role of school organization and structure. *American Educational Research Journal, 40*(2), 353–393.

Lee, V., Croninger, R., & Smith, J. (1997). Course taking, equity, and mathematics learning: Testing the constrained curriculum hypothesis in U.S. secondary schools. *Educational Evaluation and Policy Analysis, 19*(2), 99–121.

Lee, V., & Ready, D. (2007). *Schools within schools: Possibilities and pitfalls of high school reform.* New York, NY: Teachers College Press.

Meier, D. (2002). *The power of their ideas: Lessons for America from a small school in Harlem.* Boston, MA: Beacon Press.

Shear, L., Means, B., Mitchell, K., House, A., Gorges, T., Oshi, A., Smerdon, B., & Shkolnik, J. (2008). Contrasting paths to small-school reform: Results of a 5-year evaluation of the Bill & Melinda Gates Foundation's National High Schools Initiative. *Teachers College Record, 110*(9), 1986–2039.

Solórzano, D., & Ornelas, A. (2002). A critical race analysis of advance placement classes: A case of educational inequality. *Journal of Latinos and Education, 1*(4), 215–229.

Spradley, J. (1980). *Participant observation.* Orlando, FL: Harcourt, Brace, & Jovanovich.

Stanton-Salazar, R. (2001). *Manufacturing hope and despair: The schooling and kin support networks of U.S.-Mexican youth.* New York, NY: Teachers College Press.

Valenzuela, A. (1999). *Subtractive schooling: U.S.-Mexican youth and the politics of caring.* Albany: State University of New York Press.

Reflecting on Classroom-Based Literacy Research

Joan C. Fingon
Sharon H. Ulanoff

Classroom research, like the studies presented in this volume, can be both descriptive and reflective, showing how literacy researchers and literacy educators are interconnected and share the same goal: to improve literacy learning and teaching for all students (Duke & Martin, 2011). The classroom research presented here examines the work of those who went about conducting inquiries to capture instructional practices based on the context of schools and students they serve. Moreover, the studies contained in this volume are situated within diverse settings, highlighting the need for cultural awareness as well as understanding the needs of all students in those settings. As Cummins (1998) points out, students tend to "immerse themselves in literacy activities only when both the process and products of these activities are affirming of their developing academic and personal identities" (p. 17).

The studies presented in this volume highlight practical implications that are not always consistent with district mandates and school literacy policies and practices. The authors describe students who may not have been successful in schools yet are capable of becoming active and engaged learners. Likewise, although educational reports and the general press and media show that English language learners (ELLs) and other marginalized groups continue to score poorly on standardized tests compared to their counterparts, Dewey (1897/2009) long ago surmised that "the only true education comes through the stimulation of the child's powers by the demands of the social situations in which he finds himself" (p. 34). In essence, literacy educators and researchers look at the ideological and political issues that inform discussion surrounding the broader implications of literacy instruction by striving to teach all children. In the classrooms and schools highlighted in this volume, teachers act upon their reflective practices showing positive ways to facilitate student learning. They also provide evidence of the need to initiate change in literacy practices addressing learning conditions, language differences, instructional practices, and ideologies for all students with respect to literacy achievement. Clearly, in a democratic society, educational interventions must be designed to strengthen the literacy achievement and interactions by excluding no student.

Collectively, the authors describe how effective classroom teachers take advantage of students' funds of knowledge and the experiences they bring to school (Moll, Amanti, Neff, & Gonzales, 1992) and how those teachers routinely reflect, using research tools to ask difficult questions about their practice. As such, they present a unique opportunity to describe the context of their schools in ways to develop more complex profiles of their students to increase their growing knowledge of the lives and cultures of the students they teach in order to design appropriate teaching methodologies and curriculum (Banks et. al., 2007). Ultimately, such reflective work implies that teachers and schools may investigate, create, and critique their own responsive and responsible teaching and learning curriculum.

REFLECTING ON THE BOOK'S THEMES

Three recurring themes stand out across the various chapters. One theme suggests that rather than alienating students from their home and community, cultures, and languages, teachers should build upon the cultures and languages of students from diverse groups in order to enhance their learning (Moll & González, 2004). As ELLs tend to experience discrimination and marginalization in school and society because of their cultural, language, and behavioral differences, helping these children succeed remains a challenge (Banks, 2004). In other words, the authors demonstrate how inquiry takes place in classrooms by reflecting on their practices and making conscious decisions to change their practices in order to accommodate their learners' needs regardless of their linguistic or cultural backgrounds.

A second theme affirms the value of student differences in helping them succeed by supporting and incorporating the language and culture, particularly of Latino students, in schools as "the most viable path to their academic success" (Reyes & Halcon, 2001, p. 246). As such, the authors provide opportunities to investigate and create learning environments in which instruction is enriched, the academic achievement of marginalized students is enhanced, and the education of all students is improved. In other words, the authors support the notion that a good education requires education about diversity in a diverse environment (Bowen & Bok, 1998). However, the road to implementing change is often bumpy along the way and effective literacy teachers particularly working with diverse students envision their classrooms as sites of struggle and transformative action in the service of academic literacy development and social change (Banks et. al., 2007).

Lastly, and perhaps the most noticeable theme that echoed across the chapters, comes from Allington and Cunningham's (2002) words quoted in the introduction, "Schools are changed by the people who work in them" (p. 282). While public schools are influenced by political, economic, and societal needs, it is classroom teachers such as these highlighted in this book that are in the forefront of such complex situations and tensions that holds the most promise for initiating change. Recognizing that teachers have the potential to interact with others and function as change agents in their classrooms, schools, and communities requires meaningful dialogue, collaboration, and negotiation among all participants to improve schools particularly serving diverse learners. Toward these ends, through praxis, the combination of active reflection and reflective action (Freire, 1970), teachers and schools have the opportunity to build and strengthen collective efforts toward individual and social transformation.

MAKING CHANGE

To further thinking about the need for change in how students' literacy needs are being met and to assist schools and educators in conceptualizing and planning their own classroom research agenda, we make the following suggestions:

- Allocate adequate funding and ongoing professional development to ensure that the quality of teaching is equitable, especially for those working in culturally and linguistically diverse schools.
- Provide support with funding resources and materials that consider a school's unique culture and population.

- Promote opportunities for teachers to develop a culture of inquiry ethic to improve and inform their teaching practices in ways that help students learn best.
- Develop effective and safe learning environments for all students who struggle with literacy.
- Remove punitive and damaging consequences related to federal mandates and school policies that do not promote good teaching and learning.

The literacy educators and researchers included in this book describe classrooms where literacy and learning are encouraged and respected, making valuable contributions to the growing body of knowledge of effective literacy pedagogy and instructional practices. More important, this anthology speaks to empower all educators interested in engaging in professional conversations related to the process of how classroom literacy research works and to explore the complex ways in which instructional contexts support achievement for diverse classrooms.

REFERENCES

Allington, R. L., & Cunningham, P. M. (2002). *Schools that work: Where all children read and write.* Boston, MA: Allyn & Bacon.

Banks, J. A. (Ed.). (2004). *Diversity and citizenship education: Global perspectives.* San Francisco, CA: Jossey-Bass.

Banks, J. A., Au, K. H., Ball, A. F., Bell, P., Gordon, E. W., Gutiérrez, K. D., Zho, M. (2007). *Learning in and out of school in diverse environments.* Seattle, WA: LIFE Center and Center for Multicultural Education. Retrieved from http://life-slc. org/docs/Banks_etal-LIFE-Diversity-Report.pdf

Bowen, W. G., & Bok, D. (1998). *The shape of the river: Long-term consequences of considering race in college and university admissions.* Princeton, NJ: Princeton University Press.

Cummins, J. (1998). *Linguistic and cognitive issues in learning to read in a second language.* Paper presented at the Conference on Reading and English Language Learner, California Reading Project, Sacramento, CA.

Dewey, J. (2009). My pedagogic creed. In D. Flinders & S. Thorton (Eds.), *The curriculum studies reader* (pp. 34–41). New York, NY: Routledge. (Original work published 1897)

Duke, N. K., & Martin, N. M. (2011). 10 things every literacy educator should know about research. *The Reading Teacher, 65*(1), 9–22.

Freire, P. (1970). *Pedagogy of the oppressed.* New York, NY: Continuum.

Moll, L. C., Amanti, C., Neff, D., & Gonzales, N. (1992). Funds of knowledge for teaching: Using a qualitative approach to connect homes and classrooms. *Theory Into Practice, 31,* 132–141.

Moll, L. C., & González, N. (2004). Engaging life: A funds-of-knowledge approach to multicultural education. In J. A. Banks & C. A. M. Banks (Eds.), *Handbook of research on multicultural education* (2nd ed., pp. 699–715). San Francisco, CA: Jossey-Bass.

Reyes, M. de la L., & Halcón, J. J. (Eds.) (2001). *The best for our children: Critical perspectives on literacy for Latino students.* New York, NY: Teachers College Press.

About the Editors
and the Contributors

Joan C. Fingon, a professor of Reading and Education at California State University–Los Angeles, teaches in the MA in Education, Option in Reading Program, and the EdD Program in Educational Leadership. She serves as the university's literacy faculty council representative for the California State University Center of Advancement for Reading and is president of Inter-Cities Literacy Association, a local council of the California Reading Association affiliated with the International Reading Association. Her interests include classroom research in literacy and assessment and advocating for empowering teachers to promote literacy for all students. Fingon has authored many articles in scholarly journals and newsletters; this is her first coedited book publication.

Sharon H. Ulanoff, a professor of Bilingual/Multicultural and Literacy Education at California State University–Los Angeles, currently serves as the associate director of the EdD Program in Educational Leadership and also teaches in the MA in Education, Option in Reading Program. Ulanoff's research interests include literacy and biliteracy acquisition, teacher identity development, narrative inquiry, and practitioner research and assessment. Her recent publications address professional development, second language teaching, and effective second language literacy practices. She is a frequent presenter at state, national, and international conferences, and is presently a member of the editorial board of the *Bilingual Research Journal*.

Josephine Arce, a professor of Literacy and Bilingual Education, teaches in the Master of Arts: Concentration in Language and Literacy, Reading Specialists, and the Multiple Subject CLAD and BCLAD Programs at San Francisco State University. Her areas of expertise are in literacy theories, research, and practices. She is deeply committed to understanding and applying critical pedagogy and transformative processes in public schools through participatory and self-study research designs.

Diane Brantley, an associate professor in the College of Education at California State University–San Bernardino, comes to the university setting with 11 years of elementary school teaching experience. She acts as the coordinator of the Reading and Language Arts Graduate Program and oversees the Watson and Associates Literacy Center. Much of her research has been done in the field of literacy and language acquisition.

Sandra A. Butvilofsky, a professional research associate at the BUENO Center at the University of Colorado–Boulder, teaches graduate-level courses and is the director of the Colorado Literacy Squared Research Project. Butvilofsky also has experience as a bilingual classroom teacher and a trained Descubriendo la Lectura/Reading Recovery teacher. Her research interests include classroom-based research in bilingual contexts with a focus on Spanish and English writing development of bilingual Latino elementary children.

Susan Courtney, a multiage educator, currently teaches at an elementary school in Los Angeles and has dedicated more than 31 years to teaching and learning. She holds two MA degrees in Education and Curriculum and Instruction, a Reading and Language Arts Specialist Credential, and multiple certifications as a National Board Certified Teacher. Presently, Courtney is researching the role of discourse and improved teacher practice in mathematics with a network of colleagues as part of a teacher-initiated inquiry project grant.

Gregory J. Cramer, a bilingual social studies teacher, has been working in the Milwaukee Public School system for 11 years. He helped found and manage a small bilingual high school dedicated to promoting high levels of student achievement through bilingualism and biliteracy. Cramer has also taught English-as-a-second-language and literature, served as band and drama coach, and developed a schoolwide sustained silent reading program. He received his PhD in Education from the University of Wisconsin, Milwaukee in 2012.

Elizabeth Padilla Detwiler currently teaches in the Language and Literacy Masters and Reading Specialist Program at San Francisco State

University. She also has experience teaching third grade and eighth-grade humanities in a small school in the Tenderloin neighborhood of San Francisco. Her interests include connecting with other teachers and developing new ideas and theories around teaching struggling middle school readers.

Virginia Gonzalez, a professor in the School of Education at the University of Cincinnati, has a wide and varied interdisciplinary professional and academic background. Her areas of expertise are the development of multidisciplinary models explaining cognitive, linguistic, and cultural factors affecting assessment and instruction in bilingual/English-as-a-second-language (ESL), low-socioeconomic status, Latino pre-K–Grade 12 students.

Dana L. Grisham, retired professor of Literacy Teacher Education in the California State University system, presently serves as Core Adjunct Professor at National University. She is coeditor of *The California Reader,* published by the California Reading Association, and a blog author of LiteracyBeat. She has over 70 publications to her credit and believes that teaching is the most important profession in our society. Grisham's research interests include the intersections of teacher education in literacy, technology, and multiple literacies, and multicultural education.

Shira Lubliner, an associate professor at California State University–East Bay, coordinates the teacher performance assessment program, teaches graduate-level reading courses, and conducts classroom-based research in local elementary schools. She has been an educator for more than thirty years, working as a classroom teacher, principal, and teacher educator. Lubliner is an author of numerous articles and several books, including *A Practical Guide to Reciprocal Teaching: Getting into Words: Vocabulary Instruction That Strengthens Comprehension;* and *Nourishing Vocabulary.*

Jodene Kersten Morrell, a senior research associate and affiliate of the Department of Curriculum and Teaching at Teachers College, Columbia University, teaches courses and advises students in the Literacy Specialist Program. Morrell previously served as an associate professor at California State Polytechnic University–Pomona, teaching literacy courses for K–12 credential candidates and advising students in the masters program. She is the author of many book chapters and articles.

Sandra Liliana Pucci, an associate professor of linguistics at the University of Wisconsin–Milwaukee, coordinates the Adult/University-Level TESOL Certificate Program at her institution and teaches courses in bilingualism, second language acquisition, and sociolinguistics. She is the recipient of various bilingual teacher development grants from the U.S. Department of Education, as well as Refugee Teacher Training awards from the Department of Health and Human Services. Dr. Pucci currently serves on the executive board of directors of the Alliance for Multilingual and Multicultural Education (AMME). Her research interests are in the development of bilingualism and biliteracy in speakers of heritage languages.

Alice Quiocho, a retired professor of Literacy Instruction at California State University–San Marcos, specializes in reading and language instruction for ELLs. Quiocho has 42 years of experience in education including serving as director of the North County Professional Development Federation, a department of the San Diego County Office of Education; the coordinator of professional development for a K–8 public school district and the coordinator of library/media services for another K–8 district; and also as a principal, reading specialist, and teacher at the elementary and middle school levels. She coauthored her first book, *Differentiating Literacy Instruction for English Language Learners,* with Sharon H. Ulanoff.

Ambika G. Raj, associate professor of Storytelling and Language Arts at California State University–Los Angeles, teaches courses on storytelling, children's literature, preschool literacy, and educational drama, and coordinates the MA in Education, Option in Creative Literacies and Literature, and the Storytelling Certificate programs. Her research interests include arts in education, film, children's literature, and bilingual/multicultural education. She recently authored *Multicultural Children's Literature: A Critical Issues Approach.*

Richard Rogers, a multiage teacher, has taught for the past 17 years at an elementary school in Los Angeles. He has been facilitating learning for 22 years, including teaching kindergarten and physical education, and has been both a mentor and master teacher for local districts and colleges and a presenter at conferences locally and nationally. Rogers is working with Susan Courtney researching the role of talk and effective practices leading to improved student learning and achievement.

Index

DATE DUE

	PRINTED IN U.S.A.